PRINT

The Mutat
of Publishi
since 189

Alessandro Ludovico

ONOMATOPEE 77

CONTENTS

Newspaper extinction timeline, 2011

Introduction.

We've all heard the news: print is dead. Every year, declining readership and advertisement sales are forcing hundreds of well-established newspapers and magazines out of business, while employment figures within the industry have fallen back to mid-1950s levels.[1] At the same time, (independent) bookshops are withering and falling like so many autumn leaves. Digital publishing, on the other hand, is now a booming business, with traditional publishers embracing every new standard or technology in an often desperate effort to impress their sceptical shareholders. And the market for reading devices and platforms is beginning to get very crowded indeed, while digital versions of every imaginable printed material are distributed online with ever-increasing ease and speed. Online news distribution is also clearly spiralling out of control, which is why a recent April Fools' Day hoax by the internationally esteemed British newspaper, the *Guardian*, announcing that it would henceforth be publishing its news exclusively through Twitter, could sound even remotely plausible...

And yet, there are still plenty of newsstands and bookshops around, well-stocked with a wide variety of printed products. And if you are reading these words on paper (which you probably are) then you have, for some reason, chosen to go with the 'old' medium. Why? Probably because it still comes with the very best 'interface' ever designed.

So is print really dead? Is it going to die anytime soon? In this book, we shall be examining a particular (and often puzzling) period in the history of print – starting with the moment its death was first announced (already quite a long time ago, as we shall see) up to the present day, as new digital technologies are rapidly transforming both the status and the role of printed materials.

There are many different and often contradictory signals to be considered here, but it is crucial to see them within a historical perspective, as well as in the context of the most current developments. We shall attempt here to collect and systematise as many of these signals as space allows – examining various technologies, experiments, and visionary works of art, as well as hard facts and figures. The traditional role of print is unmistakeably being threatened by the new digital world; but it is also, paradoxically, being revitalised. Both media share a certain number of characteristics, and yet they are fundamentally different – and they also fulfil different needs (for example, digital is built for speed, while print ensures stability).

The two media are clashing as well, resulting in efforts from both sides to discover some ideally balanced publishing 'nirvana', where pixels and paper live together in a perfect symbiosis, generating (of course) an endless flow of revenue for everyone involved. In an effort to reach this utopian goal, publishers of all shapes and sizes are currently developing and investing in countless hybrid strategies and products: strange beasts which incorporate, either literally or conceptually, elements and qualities of both paper and pixels, in an effort to score the highest possible degree of customer satisfaction – and thus revenue. But, being hybrids, these strategies and products face an uphill struggle to be accepted, let alone embraced – and in order to do so, they must quickly find their own role and niche within the global marketplace.

As they struggle for survival, they must rapidly evolve and adapt to an ever-changing media environment. One direct consequence of this process, obviously, is that printed publishing will never be the same again: it is being deeply transformed by two opposite (even contradictory) needs. On one hand, the timeless and immutable printed page is itself increasingly subjected to a variety of real-time updating schemes. On the other hand, having an information carrier which is physically reliable (as well as independent of electrical and data connections) is increasingly being recognised as a precious resource by a generation which spends much of its days glued to 'unsteady' laptops.

The timeless 'interface' of the printed page (including its classic 'golden ratio' dimensions and 'portrait' or vertical orientation) has finally been adopted by digital publishing; on the other hand, printed products increasingly attempt to incorporate 'digital' characteristics – such as updateability and searchability. And yet, enlightening as it may be to observe such seemingly convergent developments, this is only the first step towards fully understanding this ongoing process.

We shall begin by examining more closely the so-called 'death of paper' – something which obviously has yet to happen, and which has in fact been announced more than once, starting in the late 19th century (at the time when the first public electricity networks were being developed in urban areas). The first chapter – *The death of paper (which never happened)* – chronologically analyses seven particularly representative cases which have occurred since that first defining moment. Essentially, any new medium always claims to possess characteristics superior to those of printed paper, and thus to be in a position to potentially supplant it. And yet, not a single one of these media has ever managed to seriously threaten print's dominance of its native market, or its deeply rooted status as a universal medium. Perhaps this is all about to change, with the arrival of the newest generation of mobile devices interconnected through wireless networks? Perhaps. Nevertheless, the overblown tone in which the death of the paper medium is currently being announced, should give us reason to pause and consider more closely the qualities and drawbacks of the currently emerging digital alternatives – and also how print, instead of disappearing, may instead adapt and evolve, as it has already done several times before. Historically, the unchangeable, static nature of the printed medium has always been the main justification for declaring it to be obsolete. Paradoxically, it is this very immutability of paper which is now increasingly proving to be an advantage rather than a weakness, particularly in the context of an ever-changing (thus ephemeral) digital publishing world. At the same time, there can be no doubt that the role of printed paper within the media landscape will have to be thoroughly redefined.

But to help us avoid repeating earlier mistakes, or impulsively embracing experimental developments whose time has yet to come, the second chapter – *A history of alternative publishing reflecting the evolution of print* – offers an analysis of the strategic use of print, by avant-garde artistic movements throughout the 20th century, as well as in the context of the underground press from the 1950s through the 1980s, and finally in light of the most recent developments in underground publishing (such as the production of technically perfect 'fakes' made possible through digital technology). The actions, gestures, and strategies of all of these types of press, while demonstrating how print can be put to use as a 'liberating' medium, are also intimately connected to contemporaneous technological developments. Such a parallel history of technologies and artistic strategies reveals how cultural and social passions have always found their way into print, using whatever means happened to be available and appropriate at the time – thus significantly reflecting and documenting the historical period in which they existed. Even now this continues to be the case (although in a more 'scattered' way than before, across different cultural scenes and using various combinations of technologies and strategies). As it will hopefully continue to be in the future.

Whenever some newer and more powerful technology seems ready to transform the established rules of any system, then the whole system (in this case, the media landscape) will gradually respond to the challenge. The third chapter – *The mutation of paper: material paper in immaterial times* – explores the current mutation of the role of printed paper as a medium; why paper, an inherently 'material' medium, still makes sense in our 'immaterial' age. This new role is, of course, still in the process of being clearly and comprehensively defined. The undeniable impact of digital publishing on the print publishing economy is a key factor in this process, as the established trade mechanisms and money flows which have sustained publishing for centuries are increasingly being called into question. At this turning point, with many long-established publishing enterprises facing bankruptcy, publishers both large and small struggle to (re)invent, experiment, hybridise, and exploit (some might say squeeze the last drops out of) the unique characteristics of print, while integrating new 'digital' features – or at least some essence of these features – into the printed page. Furthermore, the rapidly maturing 'print on demand' model, besides predictably revolutionising the traditional 'vanity press' and self-publishing markets, has also made possible the publication of many experimental, historical, collaborative, updateable, and otherwise non-commercial materials. And there is of course no shortage of (often enlightening) comments by media pundits on all the new and exciting possibilities offered by these endlessly mutating media forms.

This blurring of the boundaries between paper and pixel is the topic of the fourth chapter – *The end of paper: can anything actually replace the printed page?* Here we shall critically examine the various electronic devices, strategies, platforms, successes and failures, keeping in mind that the subject we are attempting to dissect is in a state of constant flow, often radically redefined by one bold gesture of a single organisation or even individual. Here our challenge will be to track down and define the elusive thread connecting recent and ongoing developments with that 'something' which is destined to become, in the next decade or so, the stable foundation of the new digital publishing. This is, of course, a cultural phenomenon, which is affecting the world of publishing in all its dimensions: from physical distribution, to the changing nature of libraries, to the formulation of new alternative models of selling printed products. The cultural and perceptual shifts involved should not be underestimated; once we have attempted to define these, we shall once again examine how artists are busy envisioning them, conceptually as well as practically.

An important future role of paper is certainly the long-term archiving of information. Thus we must understand not only the properties of paper as an archival medium, but also what the supposed 'digital archiving' of printed materials exactly means, and how the two together are already shaping what some day will become the memory of our contemporary culture. This is the subject of the fifth chapter – *Distributed archives: paper content from the past, paper content for the future*. Some of the questions we will be asking are: is paper indeed the best container for our collective long-term memory? How could small – often personal – print archives be made available online (if not their entire content, at least their collection references) for the benefit of all those interested? How could specialised archives, which cover a variety of topics, be shared using distributed and/or peer-to-peer archiving models ('curated' by individuals and small institutions, instead of major corporations and bureaucracies)? As we examine the possibilities – and compare various industrial efforts, such as the paradigm-defining Google Books – we must understand not only how paper is likely to be used from now on, but also how the choices we make today will end up determining whether publications from the (recent) past are to become (or remain) visible or invisible in the near future.

The sixth and final chapter – *The network: transforming culture, transforming publishing* – focuses on how the network, as a cultural and technological concept, has enabled a strategic transformation, making it possible for the first time to imagine and implement credible alternatives to printed paper. Electronic books, newspapers and magazines would have been poor alternatives to paper, had they not been updatable and cross-connectable through networks. Paradoxically, the network also offers print publishing its best opportunities for survival: making it possible for publishers to team up with like-minded colleagues, to connect with potential customers, to foster a collective understanding of the unique and complementary role of paper within the new digital reality, and to implement new and sustainable 'hybrid' publishing models. And when artists use networks as a platform for critical reflection and intervention within the global distribution structure (thus playing a major role in re-conceptualising it), 'networking' also becomes synonymous with the 'sharing' of cultural products – underexposed or otherwise invisible materials, whether printed or digital. Here, the individual reputation of each (known and shared) cultural product becomes a key factor in the success of a new business model established by the network.

Finally, the *Appendix* attempts to bring the two worlds (print and digital) face to face, noting their differences and similarities, and reminding us once again of how inseparable the two really are. One hundred keywords and concepts are listed in both their digital and paper incarnations. We end with this 'conceptual slide show' in an effort to temporarily 'archive' the current state of the research process initiated with this book, which is certain to be continued elsewhere – understanding fully well that print and pixel, cellulose and electricity are finally getting married (which is of course where the real problems begin), but also that their vital and dynamic relationship should above all be seen as an important historical opportunity for a new wave of meaningful, creative and independent publishing.

CHAPTER 1

The death of paper
(which never happened).

1.1   EARLY THREATS TO THE PRINTED MEDIUM.

In our present digital era, the 'death of paper' has become a plausible concept, widely expected to materialise sooner or later. The 'digitisation of everything' explicitly threatens to supplant every single 'old' medium (anything carrying content in one way or another), while claiming to add new qualities, supposedly essential for the contemporary world: being mobile, searchable, editable, perhaps shareable. And indeed, all of the 'old' media have been radically transformed from their previous forms and modalities – as we have seen happen with records, radio and video. On the other hand, none of these media ever really disappeared; they 'merely' evolved and transformed, according to new technical and industrial requirements.

The printed page, the oldest medium of them all, seems to be the last scheduled to undergo this evolutionary process. This transformation has been endlessly postponed, for various reasons, by the industry as well as by the public at large. And so the question may very well be: is printed paper truly doomed? Are we actually going to witness an endless proliferation of display screens taking over our mediascape, causing a gradual but irreversible extinction of the printed page?

It's never easy to predict the future, but it's completely useless to even attempt to envision it without first properly analysing the past. Looking back in history, we can see that the death of paper has been duly announced at various specific moments in time – in fact, whenever some 'new' medium was busy establishing its popularity, while deeply questioning the previous 'old' media in order to justify its own existence. In such moments in history, it was believed that paper would soon become obsolete.

(Historical note: paper as a medium was first invented by the Egyptians around 3500 BC using the papyrus plant, then definitively established in China starting in the 2nd century CE, before it was combined with the revolutionary movable type print technology – first introduced, again in China using woodblocks, and later on by Gutenberg in Germany in 1455 using lead alloys).

Time and again, the established mass-media role of paper has been called into question by a number of media theorists and marketing experts, who attempted in various ways to persuade society at large to get rid of paper, and choose instead some newer and supposedly better medium. This ongoing process seems to have originated in the early 20th century, when the death of paper was predicted – probably for the first time – after centuries of daily use. The development of public electricity networks, which enabled the mass distribution of new and revolutionary media, inspired visions of a radical change in the (still two-dimensional) media landscape, following a fashionable logic of inevitable progress which lives on to this day.

White House telegraph
room, Washington, D.C.,
ca. 1906
(Peter and Cornelia Weil
Typewriter Archives)

The telegraph, introduced in the second half of the 19th century, was the first medium to enable the electrical transmission of content across long distances in real time. Despite a very low 'bandwidth' of just a few characters per second, this instant connection between faraway places completely changed the way people dealt with information, starting off the 'electric' wave of innovation which came to characterise the turn of the century. The journalist Tom Standage, writing in *The Economist*, went so far as to dub the telegraph "the Victorian Internet": "The telegraph unleashed the greatest revolution in communications since the development of the printing press".[2]

After the electric telegraph wire, the next step was the quest for what the Italian inventor Innocenzo Manzetti called the "speaking telegraph",[3] and soon enough the first telephone networks were being developed – first locally, then nationally and internationally. The 'one-to-many' mode of exclusive communication (introduced by the newspapers) was now being challenged at its very core, by the wires directly connecting voices between people's houses – that is, between rich people's houses, at least for the time being.

A uniquely futuristic vision of this changing mediascape was elaborated by Octave Uzanne and Albert Robida in their illustrated story *La fin des livres*, originally published in France in 1894 in the collection *Contes pour les bibliophiles*.[4] Uzanne wrote of a future world of publishing which would no longer rely on the 'static' printed page, delivering instead all content through voice (both live and recorded) using a platform which nowadays would best be described as 'on demand'. This wasn't radio (wireless transmission had yet to be developed and popularised), neither was it any kind of telephone broadcasting (or, as we would say in contemporary terms, 'cable radio') since it relied on live-through-wires content as well as playback of recorded content (which we would now refer to as online and offline), distributed through the then-popular (and fragile) cylinder recording medium. Robida's illustrations depicted this future world in a very imaginative and effective manner, while maintaining the distinctive graphic style of the period. The future seemed to be one of wires everywhere, spreading the content of libraries into every home as well as in public spaces.

One of the illustrations from *La fin des livres* by Octave Uzanne and Albert Robida in *Contes pour les bibliophiles*, 1895

Uzanne argued that reading causes fatigue and apathy. Words heard through the tube, on the other hand, would convey energy, and thus the gramophone must inevitably supplant the printed page. The way in which Uzanne imagined this future scenario, anticipates several contemporary issues regarding the distribution of content. Watchmakers, for example, will have designed reliable miniaturised gramophones (= iPods); the required mobile electricity (still an issue in the 21st century) is generated by harnessing the user's physical movements (one of many contemporary 'green' proposals for producing clean energy). The libraries have become "phonographoteques" (= podcast repositories), while bibliophiles are now known as "phonographophiles" (= download addicts). Furthermore, in Uzanne's vision, the author becomes his own publisher (= customised print on demand), living off the royalties of his works. Finally, city squares and crossroads now feature kiosks where people can insert a coin in order to listen to works of literature (= digital kiosks) through simple headphones which are so cheap even the poor can afford them. One of the most 'retrofuturistic' inventions is a more-or-less mobile device, filled with recordings of the author's works, which he can carry with him through the streets. Using multiple wire connections, a small neighbourhood can be 'provided' with his audio content.

As for the future of the printed page – "It will be abandoned", except perhaps for some limited use in business and private communications (actually, what we see happening nowadays is exactly the opposite: since the mid-1990s, personal communication has relied less and less on paper, except in a few formal occasions). Also, "the newspaper will go the same way", since the printed word would no longer be satisfying compared to the new audio medium – and the thrilling experience of hearing the story actually being told.

There's also a passage on health issues, specifically on the results of centuries of reading in poorly-lit conditions. Uzanne notes that, just as eye doctors flourished when journalism was invented, ear specialists will prosper in the future. He concludes: "how happy we will be not to have to read any more; to be able finally to close our eyes". The daily strain on the eyes from devouring news and essays, stories and novels, could at last be avoided as the ears absorbed the information, much faster and almost effortlessly. For Uzanne, the death of print positively meant the end of a tyranny – the liberation from a debilitating slavery of the eyes. And so the new medium (catapulting us with its new sensorial experience into a future of speed and ease) would inevitably prevail against the slow and static printed page (and its dependence on our enslaved and exhausted eyes).

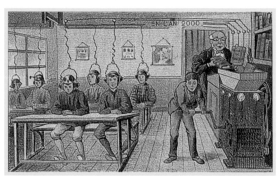

One of the postcards from the series *Villemard 1910 – en l'an 2000*, 1910

Similarly, the French artist Villemard created in 1910 a series of postcards showcasing his futuristic vision of life in Paris in the year 2000.[5] Here the concept of one medium (paper) being replaced by another (audio) is depicted even more explicitly. We see people listening to their favourite newspaper, in the form of freshly recorded cylinder phonographs played on a gramophone; the same medium is also used for personal correspondence. Schoolchildren hear their lessons through rudimentary headphones hanging from the ceiling and connected to a mysterious machine, which the teacher feeds with books, converting their content to audio through some unspecified mechanical process (somewhat resembling the grinding of meat). But although the content is converted (into immaterial sounds rather than digital bits), the supremacy of the book as the primary repository of knowledge is in itself not challenged.

1.3   *THE READIES*:
        MACHINE-READING WORDS WITHOUT PAGES.

In the early decades of the 20th century, the structural constraints of the printed page (content fixed immutably in a strictly sequential order of pages) were increasingly being perceived, after a few centuries of established use, as merely a technical limitation – something which would soon and inevitably be overcome. The avant-garde artistic and cultural movements of this period embraced the dramatic acceleration of urban daily life – the result of the industrial revolution and the increasing use and availability of electricity. Newly created requirements (speeding up processes, reconfiguring social structures, and finding new attitudes for coming to grips with these changes) affected also the printed page, a cultural symbol of the past as well as the (then) present age.

This is the background against which Bob Brown wrote his manifesto *The Readies* in 1930. Declaring that "the written word hasn't kept up with the age", Brown envisioned a completely new technology for speeding up the reading process, using strips of miniaturised text (instead of pages) scrolling behind a magnifying glass: "A simple reading machine which I can carry or move around, attach to any old electric light plug and read hundred thousand word novels in ten minutes if I want to, and I want to."

Not content with merely conceiving the technology, Brown took a first step towards its realisation, by defining a new publishing platform meant to supplant what he called the printed book's "bottled" text. One year after *The Readies*, he published *Readies for Bob Brown's Machine*, featuring texts written specifically for his new reading machine by celebrated contemporary poets such as Gertrude Stein, Filippo Tommaso Marinetti and Ezra Pound – in an experimental style reflecting the machine's structure and motion, using only indispensable words connected by hyphens and discarding the rest (such as articles and conjunctions).[6]

The Readies were meant to be more than a new form of writing – Brown envisioned a whole new medium, optically demolishing the obsolete pace of words "bottled up" in the printed page, and thus increasing the quantity of information that could be digested per unit of time (readers could control the scrolling speed according to their own personal tastes and needs): "Books are antiquated word containers (...) modern word-conveyors are needed now, reading will have to be done by machine". Impressively prophetic of the speed of the electronic word ("And words perhaps eventually will be recorded directly on the palpitating ether") and of the speed and range (and thus power) of electronic media, Brown's work also questions the relationship, in the established written forms and media, between writer and reader.

The basic technology sounds a lot like microfilm, which was then in development, and in fact Brown was in contact with some of the inventors working on prototypes. Paradoxically, this was the only form in which Brown's vision would ever be materialised – microfilm, which became a way of archiving printed content, celebrating and preserving paper and print rather than attempting to supplant them.[7]

1.4   H.G. WELLS DECLARES THE NEWSPAPER DEAD:
       UP-TO-DATE NEWS BY TELEPHONE IS THE FUTURE.

The English author Herbert George Wells is widely considered one of the spiritual fathers of science fiction (together with Jules Verne); his many works in the genre include such seminal titles as *The War of the Worlds* and *The Time Machine*. During the 1930s and 40s Wells appeared in regular radio broadcasts on the BBC, discussing "topics as diverse as world politics, the history of the printing press, the possibilities of technology and the shape of things to come".[8] Wells was a passionate believer in the essential role of the printing press in bringing knowledge to ordinary people; in a 1940 broadcast[9] he discussed the importance of print for democracy, and how the ability to read and write enables us all to become "lords and masters of our fate". And yet, only three years later (and just three years before his death), during another broadcast[10] he declared the newspaper medium to be "dead as mutton". He denounced the excessive amount of power concentrated in the hands of an unreliable press and the "prostitution" of the journalistic profession, which made it necessary to buy "three or four newspapers to find out what is being concealed from us"; he also jokingly advocated mass book burnings in order to rid local libraries of low-quality and out-of-date publications. Finally, he predicted that people would soon prefer to receive a constantly updated news summary through their telephones...

1.5   AN ATTEMPT BY RADIO TO STEAL NEWSPAPERS' LOYAL CUSTOMERS.

Within a few decades, electricity made possible first the telegraph, then the telephone, and finally radio, with its own entirely new model of broadcasting. The telegraph and the telephone were both designed to connect two single points at any given distance (in the case of the telegraph, with a slight delay between transmission and reception, but with an archival paper output; in the case of the telephone, in real time, but without any archival record). Radio, on the other hand, enabled for the first time an essentially real-time mass-media distribution of information, which until then had been the exclusive domain of big newspapers using a completely different medium. But even beyond its dynamic delivery of content, radio created in many listeners a sense of involvement, even a feeling of sensorial immersion: " 'I live right inside radio when I listen. I more easily lose myself in radio than in a book,' said a voice from a radio poll." (Marshall McLuhan, Understanding Media, 1964[11])

So it seems that the potential of voice as envisioned by Uzanne was realised thanks to radio, "with its power to turn the psyche and society into a single echo chamber" (McLuhan, Understanding Media[12]). But here again, the predicted catastrophic consequences for the printed page simply did not happen. In the 1940s, in particular (a period when radio was more popular than ever and still gaining momentum) newspapers nevertheless went on increasing their circulation. Customers seemed to enjoy the ritual of buying the morning (and often also the evening) editions from their favourite newsstands. And yet, during this period, the debate continued about how radio news was destined to inevitably supplant newspapers.

Then, in 1945 in Manhattan, a series of events took place which can be considered particularly significant in the social history of print. On June 30, a newspaper delivery drivers' strike broke out in New York, which was to last for 17 days.[13] A documentary funded at the time by the newspaper publishers' association showed what happened when thirteen million New York citizens were suddenly unable to buy their favourite newspaper. An early response to this development was that the radio stations doubled their news schedules, with programmes every hour, twenty-four hours a day. The whole episode was soon a national event, with Mayor Fiorello LaGuardia reading a Dick Tracy comic strip over the radio for the 'kiddies'.

On the other hand, many newspaper customers reacted to the strike by phoning the newspapers, who reassured them that they were still being published daily, and that people could still obtain a copy by going themselves to the newspapers' printing presses, which loyal customers started doing. On the first day of the strike, circulation of the *Herald Tribune* plummeted to 15,000 copies, but after a massive word-of-mouth campaign, circulation was back up to 65,000 copies by the last day of the strike, "by far the greater portion of them in direct over the counter sales. The Tribune readers have taken the time and trouble to come far out of their way to get a copy of their favourite morning newspaper".[14]

Circulation of the *New York Times* rose from 38,000 on the first day of the strike to 210,000 on the final day. Other major newspapers of the period, such as the *New York Sun* and the *New York World Telegram*, also saw hundreds of customers waiting patiently outside their respective presses, in orderly queues up to 17 blocks long, for as much as two to three hours.

It seems people preferred the physical and delayed enjoyment of the printed word above the real-time radio signal, to the extent that thousands of customers were ready to spend a great deal of time and energy just to obtain their copy, instead of simply switching on the radio and waiting for the latest news update to come in through the ether. As the documentary's narrator says: "Newspapers that can be read and reread, newspapers in which the public can read all about it, in their own time, at their own convenience". Near the end of the documentary, the narrator (triumphantly) states: "Once again dramatic proof has been given that no other medium can take the place of newspapers in the lives of the people."[15]

1.6   THE 'COLD' VISUAL POWER OF TELEVISION VS.
       THE 'DEAD' BOOK AND THE 'MOSAIC' OF THE NEWSPAPER.

After the age of radio, the next technology to make its appearance in the media arena was television, with its unique, hypnotic, reality-like video streams. For our society, this was a culmination of the electric revolution that had begun with the telegraph. Television was a new medium in real time, and until the late 20th century it remained the most pervasive and predominant of all media. Marshall McLuhan's seminal analysis of a new media-innervated world, written in the 1950s and 1960s, is based upon an analysis of the various (mass) media and their changing roles in a new society which had evolved from industrial-physical relationships to an information-media relationship. As McLuhan stated:

"The term 'communication' has had an extensive use in connection with roads and bridges, sea routes, rivers, and canals, even before it became transformed into 'information movement' in the electric age. Perhaps there is no more suitable way of defining the character of the electric age than by first studying the rise of the idea of transportation as communication, and then the transition of the idea from transport to information by means of electricity."[16]

The mass scale achieved by television in the 1960s gave it an unassailable position in all industrialised nations, reflecting the emerging 'global village' through an electric (and thus instantaneous) distribution of information – in striking contrast with the centuries-old model of the physical printed page, which seemed unable to compete because of its physical limitations. The shared feeling of 'global interconnectedness' through a real-time video transmission was something the printed page had never been able to provide. At this point in history, as a fascination with speed and progress was transforming people's perception of time and space, the printed medium seemed simply too slow to allow information to be simultaneously diffused and consumed.

McLuhan, the most visionary of mass-media theorists, spent his life analysing media. His famous division of 'cold' and 'hot' media assigned to print a very low potential for audience participation: "typography as a hot medium involves the reader much less than did manuscript", while on the other hand "TV as cool media involve(s) the user, as maker and participant, a great deal."[17] He regarded the book as no longer adequate in this new age of speed and electricity, and thus ultimately doomed:

"It is the almost total coverage of the globe in time and space that has rendered the book an increasingly obsolete form of communication. The slow movement of the eye along lines of type, the slow procession of items organized by the mind to fit into these endless horizontal columns – these procedures can't stand up to the pressures of instantaneous coverage of the earth."[18]

McLuhan was sharply criticised for his determination to discredit the book as a valid form of media. Harry J. Boyle, writing in the *Ottawa Citizen*, commented: "He was ridiculed for saying that books were dead even as he used them to convey his ideas. Actually he never said that books were dead but rather that they had been nudged from their central role by other media."[19] Nevertheless, McLuhan had an entirely different opinion of newspapers and magazines, noting how they flourished after the arrival of the new TV medium: "One of the unexpected effects of TV on the press has been a great increase in the popularity of Time and Newsweek. Quite inexplicably to themselves and without any new effort at subscription, their circulations have more than doubled since TV." And even more importantly: "If telegraph shortened the sentence, radio shortened the news story, and TV injected the interrogative mood into journalism."[20]

In fact, the new globalisation process was gradually incorporating print as well, and transforming it once again. Full-page facsimile transmission of international newspapers over long distances, which began in the 1960s and was upgraded in the following decades using dedicated satellite links, allowed newspapers to overcome the problem of shipping delays by printing remotely in different places at the same time. This new and forced evolution of print, along with its role of reflecting the uncertainty of a rapidly changing world (whether in the pondered style of the book, or the freeze-frame of the newspaper) is actually what allowed it to survive. Furthermore the stable, archival role of the printed page, and its potential for endless and exact duplication (qualities dismissed by McLuhan) were powerful features, especially in contrast with the volatility of the upcoming electronic media. Print never failed to reach its faithful audience, whether in the closed and portable form of a book, or in the 'mosaic'[21] and dynamic form of a newspaper or magazine.

1.7   COMPUTERS VIRTUALISING PAPER:
       THE 'PAPERLESS' PROPAGANDA.

At some point in history, someone may well have asked: *What's wrong with paper?*. It's no accident that this is the title of the second chapter of a book by Abigail J. Sellen and Richard H. R. Harper called *The Myth of the Paperless Office*,[22] about paper and its place in office life. From the very beginning, paper has always played a predominant role in the office. Historically, even Thomas Alva Edison, attempting to envision a practical use for his early experiments in recording on cylinders, saw them as a 'paper-reducing' (as opposed to 'paper-replacing') medium. The cylinders, wrapped in their thin aluminium foils, would contain spoken letters and memos to be shipped to their recipients, thus reducing paper use and speeding up the writing and typing process.[23]

Vannevar Bush, in the context of his complex *Memex* system, also imagined microfilm (used as the first alternative medium for 'virtualising' paper) as a means of mass storage and retrieval, reducing space and making data searchable using computers and cameras. And the limits of paper were also addressed in the early decades of computer science by J.C.R. Licklider in his famous book *Libraries of the Future*, published in 1965. Licklider sketched a futuristic impression of computer-based technologies (including pen input and speech recognition) combined in order to make information easily searchable, and to overcome the inescapable limitations of paper, mainly its size and weight.[24]

We can trace the actual expression 'paperless office' back to an article titled *The Office of the Future*, published in *Business Week* in June 1975.[25] The second section of the article is titled *The Paperless Office*. Besides predicting how computing giants (IBM and Xerox) would dominate the office market until the end of the century, this section looks into electronic methods of managing information which were expected to reduce, progressively but drastically, the amount of paper used in the working environment. The section begins with a quote from George E. Pake, then head of Xerox Corp.'s Palo Alto Research Center (PARC):

> "(...) in 1995... I'll be able to call up documents from my files on the screen... I can get my mail or any messages. I don't know how much hard copy (printed paper) I'll want in this world."

Starting in the early 1980s (the beginning of the age of personal information) this 'paperless' research-and-development mantra would increasingly become a propaganda buzzword aimed at creating a large target market for selling information technology (IT). Marketing departments actively promoted a vision of massive magnetic archiving systems, destined to replace the huge amounts of messy paper, effectively de-cluttering the desktop once and for all. This meant a definitive shift towards systems of digital documents, existing only in windows on computer screens.

But every IT user sooner or later experiences some substantial data failure – and this unavoidable 'IT error' paradigm effectively undermines any possible faith in an entirely digital model. It was also a historical miscalculation to consider this 'virtualisation' process solely from a perspective of digital production, instead of attempting to understand how to enhance well-established paper-based dynamics. What all the propaganda aimed to evoke – the eradication of the jungle of paper from the clean and orderly industrial interface – was thus undermined by the instability of the new technology, as well as people's familiarity with paper-based communication methodologies.

Sellen and Harper deconstruct the 'paperless' propaganda, stating that: "We have heard stories of paperless offices, but we have never seen one. (...) For example in one organization, managers banned the use of personal filing cabinets, only to find that people resorted to using their car or home offices to store their paper files." In fact, it should be noted that 'paperless' has remained a recurring propaganda theme ever since – promising to not only get rid of unwanted stacks of paper, but also (and perhaps more fundamentally) to reclaim physical space.

But the types of interaction made possible by paper are not yet available through new technologies (nor vice-versa, for that matter). There is still no electronic device which reproduces all the characteristics of paper: being lightweight, foldable, manipulable according to various reading activities, easily shareable with a small group of people interacting with each other simultaneously using a single medium, and being able to easily contain very different types of content, all instantly generated by hand, or juxtaposed with prepared (reproduced) content.

In fact, it seems much easier to digitally simulate the limitations of paper than its strengths – and this is unlikely to change any time soon. For example, the 'readability' of paper seems very important to us: most people still choose to print a long document and read it on paper, rather than read it on a screen. So not only did the paperless office fail to happen, but the production and use of paper, both personal and work-related, and generally speaking the printed medium, have actually increased in volume. Paradoxically, paper has even significantly contributed to spreading the culture and consciousness of the new media. Paper is persistent, as is the ink printed upon it. Printed paper stays around for a very long time, and its content doesn't change at the click of a button. Furthermore, we have the experience of a few thousand years of practice in reading externally illuminated paper. Since the 1990s, paper documents, rather than simply being supplanted by their electronic alter egos, are instead finding new ways to interact with them. So again: what's wrong with paper?

1.8   HYPERTEXT, SOMETHING PAPER CAN'T BE.

The way we deal with reading and writing practices has in fact been literally revolutionised, not so much by a new medium, but rather by a new concept implemented within a new medium. It's not the computer itself which has forever changed the linearity of text – it's the possibility, through software, of creating in the abstract digital space a functional, entirely new text structure: the hypertext. Starting in the mid-1980s, the arrival of offline hypertexts signalled a radical change, which was to have a profound effect on the concept of the literary work. In fact, the hypertext enabled the realisation of an essential new characteristic: non-linearity of text. The consequence of this was a existential threat to the integrity of the sequential work, as it had been presented for centuries in books. And even though literature is still the main field for experimentation and innovation in print, the arrival of the hypertext enabled, perhaps for the very first time, a characteristic which could not effectively be reproduced in print.

Robert Coover clearly and authoritatively described this phenomenon in his seminal essay *The End of Books*: "Print documents may be read in hyperspace, but hypertext does not translate into print",[26] and so the endlessly deep narrative space made possible by the hypertext seemed destined to supplant the finite, sequential and closed format of books, eventually making them altogether obsolete. According to Coover, the 'superior' form of the hypertext brings "true freedom from the tyranny of the line" – particularly so in the case of narrative-based text. When the boundless cultural space of the 'hypertextual' global Web is finally opened up, will the printed page by comparison start to look like so much yellowed paper?

The acclaimed Spanish author Jorge Luis Borges imagined such a dizzyingly endless text, in his 1975 short story *The Book of Sand*: a book with no beginning or end, its pages numbered, apparently uniquely but following no discernible pattern, so that the reader can never find the first or last page (the book was purchased from a bookseller who acquired it in exchange for a handful of rupees and a Bible, from an owner who did not know how to read).[27]

In his essential 1994 book *Hyper/Text/Theory*, George P. Landow said of the hypertext phenomenon: "It promises (or threatens) to produce effects on our culture, particularly on our literature, education, criticism and scholarship, just as radical as those produced by Gutenberg's movable type."[28] The digital technology then begins to radically alter the way in which we read, as the Brazilian media artist Giselle Beiguelman explored in a 1999 online artwork called *O Livro depois do Livro* ('The Book after the Book'). The different roles assumed by the machine ('reader' in the case of browser software, 'writer' in text-generating software, and 'interface' between reader and text) are here theoretically and functionally integrated. In Beiguelman's own words: "From screen to screen, the letter migrates, de-contextualises itself, making of language an aesthetic problem."[29]

And yet, despite its widespread use and incontestably tremendous potential (an early hypertext system for the authoring of technical manuals was appropriately called *PaperKiller*[30]), the hypertext has not yet succeeded in supplanting the 'traditional' text. The development of various 'wiki' platforms has dramatically expanded the hypertext's possibilities for collective authorship and the compilation of resources. It's clear that the hyperlink is now definitely embedded in our culture – on the other hand, the concept and implementation of hyperlinks are extremely computer-specific and unrelated to any established procedure used in traditional writing and publishing. We're nowhere close to hypertexts replacing the printed page in the way Robert Coover envisioned: "Indeed, the very proliferation of books and other print-based media, so prevalent in this forest-harvesting, paper-wasting age, is held to be a sign of its feverish moribundity, the last futile gasp of a once vital form before it finally passes away forever, dead as God."[31]

And yet, less than two decades later, books and magazines (whether traditional or in some mutated form) still abound; the most dramatic effect of the hypertext seems to be the way it enables the development of extraordinary new resources, with profound repercussions on a number of specific types of publishing. In this sense Katherine Hayles seems to have forecast much more accurately the future development of trends which were already emerging as she was working on her book *Writing Machines*: "A print encyclopedia qualifies as a hypertext because it has multiple reading paths, a system of extensive cross-references that serve as a linking mechanism, and chunked text in entries separated typographically from one another."[32]

If this sounds like the perfect background for the development of Wikipedia, it should be noted that Wikipedia itself has recently implemented a new functionality for generating traditional 'printed page' layouts for its entries.[33] (On the other hand, the makers of the *Encyclopedia Britannica* announced in 2012 that they would be discontinuing their expensive and bulky print edition, after 244 years – though Encyclopedia Britannica, Inc is still very much in business, specifically in the fields of educational publishing and online educational tools.[34])

1.9   THE DEATH OF PAPER... HAS YET TO HAPPEN.

So the death of paper – in retrospect, one of the most unfortunate and embarrassing prophecies of the information age – has obviously not happened. Various kinds of printed pages are still being produced in huge quantities, and globally distributed, on a mass scale as well as on a very personal level. Nevertheless, the role of the printed page has radically mutated, from being a prevalent medium in its own right, to being a complementary medium, sometimes used as a static repository of electronic content.

The printed page has become more valuable, less expendable. This is because the duplication processes associated with paper are still limited and costly, and take up both space and time. Making a physical copy of a book involves either reproducing it page by page – or printing it from a digital file, again page by page. The result is a stack of paper occupying a significant physical space, and space seems to have become one of the most valuable resources in our consumption-oriented age.

Electricity, radio, TV, computers and the World Wide Web have all affected, transformed and revolutionised the printed medium in various ways; still, our attachment to the particular characteristics of paper remains more or less intact. Nevertheless, networks are radically changing the way paper is produced and consumed. Editors, for example, must now select their printed content much more carefully, because of the huge amount of free content available online.

Actually, paper and pixel seem to have become complementary to each other; print is increasingly the medium of choice for preserving the 'quintessence' of the Web. The editor of printed material is the curator, the human filter, the one who decides what should be saved on a stable medium, and what should be left as a message in a bottle tossed into the sea of the Internet. So the printed page, with its sense of unhurried conclusiveness, allows to the reader to pause, to reflect, to take notes, without having to rely on electricity. And paper is also being used to preserve a substantial part of the digital culture, independently of hardware or software, describing the new media from the technical perspective of an old medium.

CHAPTER 2

A history of alternative publishing reflecting the evolution of print.

2.1   PRINT IS LIBERATING.

As André Breton, one of the founders of the 1920s Surrealist art movement, famously declared: "One publishes to find comrades!"[35] This short statement brilliantly embodies the spirit of early avant-garde publishing, as well as that of independent publishing later in the 20th century. Strictly speaking, the main concern here is neither commercial success, nor the aesthetic purity of the printed experiment, nor even the archiving of works (at least not yet). Rather, this kind of publishing is all about fostering and spreading ideas among like-minded people, through the 'viral' communication model so often applied by the alternative press.

(Left to right)
André Breton, René
Hilsum, Louis Aragon
and Paul Eluard, with
Dada #3, circa 1920

But when did this 'alternative' concept come into existence? Actually, it predates even Gutenberg, going at least all the way back to when the 'Biblia Pauperum' were being printed in woodcut. These were single-sheet illustrations of passages from the Bible, rendered in a style which today would best be described as comic strips, in an attempt to reduce the complexity of the original text into something more 'popular', a phenomenon which was mostly ignored by the educated elite of the time.[36]

Later, Gutenberg's movable type print itself turned out to be the

Example of a 'Biblia Pauperum' woodcut, 1470

'media technology' invention which facilitated the spread of the Protestant Reformation.[37] By making the original text of the Bible accessible to anybody with a printed copy, it became possible for individuals to decide for themselves the meaning of the scriptures, based on their own reading. This new practice was called 'self-salvation' (and in a way, the spread of Gutenberg's printing press also meant the beginning of self-publishing).

Another case in point is the body of work of the Ranters, a radical group which flourished during the second half of the 17th century, with heretical views on religion (if Jesus is in everyone, who needs the Church?), politics (expropriation of the rich and collective ownership of property) and sex (preaching an ideal of free love). Such an extremist rebel group (which counted a few thousand followers in London alone) could easily self-publish and distribute its pamphlets. Though such

publications were banned and burned, it was much more difficult to destroy an entire printed edition than had been the case with manuscripts, because of the sheer number of copies as well as their widespread distribution – and so some copies survived, a few even to this day.[38]

The Ranters Ranting, a newssheet about the Ranters, 1650

The two major political revolutions of the 18th century were both preceded by a frenzy of intellectual self-publishing activity, including a few 'underground' bestsellers. In the case of the French Revolution, many of the countless pamphlets produced were sponsored by printers, based on their potential commercial success. And at the beginning of the American Revolution, in 1776, Thomas Paine became famous for (anonymously) publishing a uniquely popular pamphlet (with a circulation of hundreds of thousands of copies) titled *Common Sense*, which provided the intellectual spark for the uprising. Paine was

Thomas Paine's pamphlet *Common Sense*, 1792

a prolific pamphleteer, as well as an early independent publisher. During the same period, it should be noted, the eminent British poet William Blake self-published all his works, including his now-famous masterpieces. But independent publishing, from the late 18th century onwards, was still mostly a medium used for spreading the kind of dissident political ideas which would eventually inspire the Mexican and Russian revolutions in the early 20th century – just as a multitude of new and extraordinary artistic and cultural movements was beginning to emerge.

2.2   THE USE OF PRINT IN THE 20TH CENTURY AVANT-GARDE.

In the early 20th century, the introduction of electricity was rapidly transforming urban daily life as well as the media landscape. And so the various emerging avant-garde art movements envisioned a brave new world, driven not only by electricity itself, but also by industry and the new upcoming media, all of which were seen as tools for conceptually revolutionising the existing order.

The first art movement to attempt this transformation was Italian Futurism, with its hostility towards the perceived mawkishness of Romanticism, and its own eagerness to force a radical break with the past. The Futurists' bold, iconoclastic statements (to which they owed much of their original fame and cultural impact) were distributed through various channels, including of course printed media. Filippo Tommaso Marinetti was in fact quite fond of print, particularly magazines. In 1905 he was editor in chief of *Poesia*, the international journal of the Futurist movement,[39] produced with the support of a sympathetic printer – until Marinetti cancelled the project a few years later and went on to collaborate with the Florentine editor Giovanni Papini (who also worked closely with other Futurists). The resulting *Lacerba* magazine, printed in 1914, featured a re-thinking of typographical composition, beginning a process (with Marinetti's famous work *Parole in Libertà*) of pushing to the very limit the possibilities of black-and-white letterpress printing. The use of markedly contrasting font sizes, as well as a creatively graphical positioning of text elements (diagonally, forming visual patterns, etc) all helped to produce a new kind of typography, which aimed to express not only a rich variety of visual forms but also powerful emotions.[40]

A few years later Marinetti would be a key contributor to the definitive journal promoting Futurism as a cultural movement (including its unfortunate political involvement with Fascism). *L'Italia futurista*, published from 1916 to 1918, was important from a media perspective for its publication of photographic sequences of the *Teatro sintetico futurista* ('Futurist Synthetic Theatre') performances.[41] Marinetti also used print to produce propaganda leaflets: his Manifesto was printed on a two-sided leaflet, as was his response to an anonymous knife attack on the Boccioni painting *La Risata* during an exhibition. Also, in 1910 he climbed the Clock Tower in Venice to drop leaflets (fiercely condemning the city's Romantic rhetoric and cultural policy) upon the crowd below.[42]

In a more or less parallel development, the Dadaist movement from the very beginning produced various journals in different cities (Zurich, Berlin, Cologne, Amsterdam, Paris, New York, Tbilisi), which shared the distinctive Dadaist principles, while also reflecting local sensibilities. They may be seen as ancestors of the later 'zines': both are characterised by the same ephemeral nature (often going out of circulation after a single issue), and both challenge the graphic and journalistic conventions of their time, embracing instead the sheer pleasure of expressing ideas in print, in a way that reflects these ideas in content as well as graphic form. The now rare and collectable Dadaist magazine *Dada*, for example, published and designed by Tristan Tzara, which made its debut in July 1917, was printed on letterpress, stretching contemporary technical possibilities to the limit in order to reflect the Dadaists' radical approach towards interpreting and transforming contemporary society.

The Dadaists attempted to exploit the experimental possibilities of the printing machine, through a playful use of font sizes and by creatively integrating lines acting as content separators or as purely graphic elements. Later on, even collages and photomontages were created manually and reproduced mechanically, definitively breaking through the rigid grid-based order of the published page, and entering the field of artistic re-appropriation and re-contextualisation of content. Most of the Dadaist magazines were produced through the patronage of sympathetic printers, who helped get around censorship problems and generally promoted self-publishing in a way that made these printed products affordable to artists.

The Surrealist movement used print as well, most notably to produce a small number of magazines which embodied in various forms the Surrealists' playful social satire. The first was *La Révolution Surréaliste*, published from 1924 to 1929. Its first issue, edited by André Breton, was designed to closely resemble the conservative scientific review *La Nature*, thus deceiving the reader into an unexpected encounter with the Surrealists' typically scandalous content. *Documents*, a later journal edited by Georges Bataille from 1929 to 1930, featured original cover art, harsh juxtapositions of pictures and text, and generally speaking a more extreme approach (compared to Breton's 'mainstream' Surrealism, and especially compared to the art-dealer-sponsored luxurious *Minotaure* magazine, published from 1933 to 1939). In a way, all these magazines, even as they called into question the printed medium, also reflected upon this very medium (by emphasising its graphical space and the challenges inevitably posed by its technical limitations) – just as they questioned and reflected upon the historical era of transformation of which they were very much a part.

Another contemporary master in this context was El Lissitzky, with the fascinating and visionary techniques he applied to graphic space. In his *Prounen* series of drawings from the early 1920s, he created complex, purely abstract three-dimensional spaces (using only ink and paper) which now may seem like a precursor of computer graphics and their endlessly programmable possibilities. His abstract conceptions literally broke through the constraints of the printed page, reformulating the concept of space within a single sheet of paper. He also redefined the book, a popular but nevertheless iconic object, as a different kind of space: "In contrast to the old monumental art (the book) itself goes to the people, and does not stand like a cathedral in one place waiting for someone to approach... (The book is the) monument of the future."[43] Lissitzky considered the book as a dynamic object, a "unity of acoustics and optics" that required the viewer's active involvement.

An even more amazing prediction was formulated in the conclusion of his *Topography of Typography* statement, published in 1923 in

Kurt Schwitters' *Merz* magazine (see also chapter 4.4). Here Lissitzky speculated on different levels about the new characteristics of what he defined as "the book space", which would definitively break with previous conventions – and he ends with a climactic definition in capital letters: "THE ELECTRO-LIBRARY", championing a future vision of books more 'optical' and sensorial than physical, and combining this vision with the core technology of the time: electricity.

2.3   THE MIMEOGRAPH OR STENCIL DUPLICATOR,
       ENABLING UNDERGROUND PUBLISHING.

So even the exhilarating spirit of the early avant-garde could not do away with traditional printing. The avant-garde struggled with the established technology of printing, and it did so with an admirably innovative approach. But the following decades would see the appearance of new technologies and devices which were to change forever the very concept of print.

One of the most important of these devices is undeniably the stencil duplicator, also known as the mimeograph machine or 'mimeo'.

Autographic printing, a
mimeograph precursor
invented by Thomas
Alva Edison, 1876

Thomas Alva Edison patented a device for 'autographic printing' in 1876, the first step of a process that led in 1887 to the production and marketing of the mimeograph. After a slow start, this revolutionary technology was appropriated in the 1930s by left-wing radical groups (not without some ideological controversy, as this effectively meant replacing unionised print workers with a cheap, lightweight machine). Significantly, the radical trade unionists of the Industrial Workers of the World (IWW) embraced the mimeo stencil, declaring it to be the IWW's unionised printing facility. So even more than artists, it was political activists and dissidents (such as the exiled Trotsky, who printed his political 'zine' *Byulleten Oppositzii* in this way) who found in

A woman using a mimeograph machine, 1930

the mimeograph the ideal medium for fostering freedom of expression and ideas, particularly during the years before and immediately after the Second World War. The mimeograph turned out to be the ideal clandestine printing device. It was lightweight and compact enough to be easily moved from place to place, thus avoiding confiscation and censorship, while also being suitable for producing a reasonable amount of copies.[44]

In subsequent years, the mimeograph would give rise to the first major waves of alternative print publishing, in two very different contexts, reflecting the upcoming geopolitical dichotomy of the period (U.S.A. vs. U.S.S.R.). By now, the mimeograph was being marketed to offices (circulars, newsletters), schools (classroom materials) and churches (bulletins). The key selling point was that it allowed short-run productions to be made cheaply, quickly and with reasonable print quality.

But such a device was also very interesting to those wishing to create printed productions outside of mainstream print infrastructures. And so in the U.S.A. the mimeograph was used by a generation of science-fiction enthusiasts to produce a multitude of 'fanzines' (as the term was soon coined) with a peak of production in the 1950s. Despite the fragile and easily corrupted stencils, the often messy printed results and ink-stained hands, this device was essentially the first 'personal printer'. The crude aesthetic of the SF fanzines and their limited

circulation were characteristic of a scattered but prolific scene, genuinely more interested in discussing the latest productions, than in the possible socio-cultural implications of a critical glance into possible future developments of their chosen medium. Nevertheless, an extensive scene was established here, with its own distinctive characteristics – for example, a readiness to simply swap issues with each other, without anyone seeming to worry too much about who was getting the better deal. (It should also be noted in passing that *Beatitude*, the first 'zine' of the Beat movement, was also printed using the mimeograph.)[45]

During the same period, on the other side of the globe, in the post-Stalinist U.S.S.R. (and other countries with a similar socio-economic system), the same medium was being used for a completely different purpose: clandestinely copying, sharing and distributing dissident literature or other media suppressed by the government. This kind of underground printed production was called 'Samizdat' (a contraction of 'self-publication' in Russian). Often no more than a few copies were made at a time, and those who received a copy were expected to make more copies. When there was no mimeograph machine at hand, copies were made by handwriting or typing. Within the Soviet bloc, Poland and Czechoslovakia were the most active Samizdat-producing countries. In Poland, especially, alongside the hundreds of small individual publishers, several large underground publishing houses also flourished, with supplies either smuggled in from abroad or stolen from official publishing houses.[46] The perceived threat of the Samizdat phenomenon for Communist regimes was so great that the Romanian dictator Nicolae Ceausescu went so far as to forbid the possession of unmonitored typewriters by Romanian citizens.

2.4   FLUXUS, PRINTED MATERIALS CIRCULATING WITHIN AN 'ETERNAL NETWORK'.

Another art movement, arguably one of the most influential to our current communication-driven mediascape, based much of its multi-directional strategy on printed materials. In the early 1960s, George Maciunas founded his Fluxus movement, with its legendary event scores, performances and 'Fluxus boxes' filled with organised collections of games, concepts, plastic objects and miscellaneous printed materials. In these carefully designed objects, produced in limited editions that were in fact quite cheap to make, the printed components (brochures, leaflets, flip books, maps, playing cards, etc) were always an integral part of the concept.[47]

Soon, the 'Fluxus newsletters' were being published to facilitate communication and the exchange of ideas within the network of Fluxus artists spread across three continents. Maciunas also collected various newspaper cuttings of Fluxus-related articles into a 'newspaper roll' to be displayed as a kind of advertisement in public spaces.

But the most consistent effort in print by Maciunas and his associates was certainly the *Fluxus Newspaper*. The earliest issues were basically anthologies of Fluxus artists from various countries; the fourth issue, however, featured a *Fluxus Symphony Orchestra in Fluxus Concert* poster, meant to be torn apart as a way of promoting the event; the fifth issue contained a catalogue of Fluxus editions, also meant to be torn apart; and for the seventh issue, Maciunas asked artists to contribute "events related to the paper page", which were printed as two separate editions: as a regular newspaper, and on card stock.[48] The magazines were shipped in parcels to Fluxus members in various cities, who personally formed a distribution infrastructure parallel to the European Mail-Order Fluxshop already set up in Amsterdam.

Another radical Fluxus approach to print was to sell cheaply-made art books at prices usually associated with prestigious collector's editions. Several Fluxus publishing houses were founded, of which Dick Higgins' Something Else Press was probably the most well-known, pioneering the artist's book movement with book editions running anywhere between 1,500 to 5,000 copies and sold at standard bookshop prices.[49]

Several of the countless Fluxus artworks dealt with the subject of money, specifically banknotes, which are probably the most precious (and the most trusted) of all printed materials. Banknotes may also be considered as limited-edition 'original prints' – a concept which is essentially nonsense anyway, since print was invented for potentially endless serial production. Artistic imitation of banknotes is a recurring theme in art, but the Japanese Fluxus artist Genpei Akasegawa took the idea quite literally, while pushing the aforementioned 'original print' conceptual nonsense to its logical conclusion. In 1963 he commissioned a print run of 1,000 Yen banknote replicas, which he proceeded to use in his announcements and performances. Unfortunately, the following year he was arrested and convicted of currency counterfeiting. He then went on to create a series of zero-yen banknotes, as a comment on the absurdity of his trial.[50]

Finally, the Fluxus movement was also the first to properly formulate the seminal concept of the network. The 'Eternal Network' was a radical idea, enabling practices which would transform the working methods of many artists: an "ongoing, global artistic network in which each participating artist realizes that s/he is part of a wider network. It is a model of creative activity with no borders between artist and audience, with both working on a common creation." (Chuck Welch, *Eternal Network: A Mail Art Anthology*)[51]

The Eternal Network was initiated by Fluxus artists Robert Filliou and George Brecht, who introduced the concept in April 1968 in a poster mailed to several correspondents. This can be seen as one of the earliest conceptual models of an international network of artists working together through postal communication – a forerunner of what a few years later would become the Mail Art network.

The influence of Fluxus on underground print was not long in waiting. For example, *Aspen*, an experimental "multimedia magazine of the arts" published by Phyllis Johnson from 1965 to 1971 and designed by various contributing artists, featured "culture along with play": each issue came in a customised box filled with booklets, phonograph recordings, posters, postcards – one issue even included a reel of Super 8 film. Johnson herself was later quoted as saying: "We wanted to get away from the bound magazine format, which is really quite restrictive."[52]

2.5   THE UNDERGROUND PRESS BOOM,
OFFSET COLOUR DRIPPING AND THE NETWORK (AGAIN).

In the mid-1960s, new countercultural and revolutionary movements were emerging which would give rise to a further transformation of alternative print, spawning countless new magazines by the end of the decade. Probably the first important sign of things to come was the *Greenwich Village Voice*, founded in 1955 in a two-bedroom apartment in New York, and positioning itself from the start in fierce opposition to the 'bourgeois' culture of the glossy *New Yorker* magazine. For almost a decade, the *Village Voice* would remain the one and only point of reference for the radical cultural critique it embodied.

Then in September 1966, all the way on the other end of the country, the first issue of the *San Francisco Oracle* was published, giving a legitimate and superlative voice to the Haight-Ashbury counterculture, while once again revolutionising print design. Affordable offset printing had gradually improved to the point where it could now effectively reproduce the psychedelic aesthetic, originally produced using silkscreen printing. The *Oracle* was designed by Allen Cohen and his staff, who tormented the printers with endless requests for special colours, until the printers finally gave up and left the presses in the hands of Cohen and his associates so they could do it their own way. They soon started filling the various inkwells of the printing presses without paying too much attention to where any particular colour went, resulting in rainbows of colours splashed and blended all across the pages.[53]

The *Oracle* (which peaked at a print run of 150,000 copies) epitomised the idea that a magazine could be more than simply a handful of paper conveying literary and political information. By doing away with the traditional 'static' typographical structure, headlines could be designed rather than composed, and texts were no longer laid out as blocks of letters, but were allowed to penetrate the illustrations spread across multiple pages. Thus the magazine became an object to behold, an image to experience – in one word, a 'trip'.[54] This use of colour broke with the established modalities of information transmission, and the result, besides being a popular success, was also a masterly reflection of the aesthetic and the spirit of the times, soon to be imitated by countless other underground magazines. Once again, this new alternative publishing scene was able to survive through the support of a few sympathetic printers. And soon enough, the first printing cooperatives were being set up.

The geographical on-the-road 'trip' of the 1960s generation was also reflected in publishing, the best example of which is probably

Other Scenes, a bi-weekly publication edited by John Wilcock in whatever world city he happened to be at the moment, and then distributed globally.[55]

Another powerful concept (and one foreseen by Fluxus) to emerge during this period was the idea of a 'network' of magazines. In its cooperative form, this concept was brought into practice by the Underground Press Syndicate, a network of counterculture newspapers and magazines founded in 1967 by several early underground publishers. The common agreement was that any member of the network was allowed to reprint, free of charge, the contents of any other member, and that any publication could join the network later on, provided they agreed to the same terms. The result was a widespread distribution of countercultural articles, stories and comics, as well as a treasure trove of content immediately available to even the smallest startup publication. At the time it was founded, the Underground Press Syndicate brought together 62 of the approximately 150 publications then considered as underground press.

Another remarkable effort was the Liberation News Service, a left-wing alternative news service which published news bulletins from 1967 to 1981, rapidly growing from a single mimeographed sheet

Cover of *Liberation News Service* #275, 1970

distributed to ten newspapers, to a complete publication featuring 20 pages of articles and photographs, and mailed twice a week to almost 800 subscribers. Through its contacts with worldwide Western radical groups as well as Third World liberation forces, the Liberation News Service was able to draw attention to a new global perspective by documenting important facts which were either totally ignored or else poorly documented by the mainstream press.

By 1969, virtually every sizeable city or college town in North America had at least one underground newspaper. And yet, by 1973 most of them had already gone out of circulation. Still, one new publication was fostering the development of networks as well as the spreading of information. The *Whole Earth Catalog*, published by Stewart Brand regularly between 1968 and 1972, and occasionally afterwards, embraced a mission of promoting "access to tools". Brand, in his own words, wanted everyone to be able to "find his own inspiration, shape his own environment, and share his adventure with whoever is interested".[56]

While remaining, strictly speaking, a catalogue (listing a huge variety of 'tools' including maps, professional journals, courses, classes, specialised utensils, even early synthesisers and personal computers), the *Whole Earth Catalog*'s editorial selection was very sophisticated, resulting in something between a curatorial work and a list of resources. Furthermore, the listings were continually revised according to the experiences and suggestions of users as well as the staff. Thus the level of interaction and involvement between publisher and users/readers was unusually high; this 'tool' was a networked one, used for unveiling and sharing important information, and allowing people to change their relationship with their personal and social environments. The *Whole Earth Catalog*'s farewell statement in 1974 was prophetic for future generations of underground publishers: "Stay hungry, stay foolish."

2.6   PHOTOCOPYING THE WORLD,
        RE-APPROPRIATING CULTURE.

After the mimeograph stencil, the next technology destined to revolutionise underground print was xerography, also known as photocopying. This was first marketed by Xerox in the 1960s for use in offices (although the basic principle of 'electrostatic printing' had been described as far back as the 18th century). Later, in the 1970s, the technology gradually became available to the general public, through coin-operated machines or in specialised copy shops. A black-and-white copy of any original could now be created cheaply and instantaneously, opening up endless new possibilities for small-print productions.

Photocopying made its appearance just before the beginning of the mid-1970s Punk cultural revolution, which quickly and wholeheartedly embraced this new medium, for its particular aesthetic qualities as well as its properties as a means of communication. Publishing a zine, or printing a flyer, was now easier than ever. Punk zines became an integral element of the Punk culture, making full use of the medium's black-and-white aesthetic, and with a playful attitude towards the photocopying process itself (for example, the shades and contrasts obtained by re-copying a copy, the ability to 'photograph' objects placed directly upon the scanning window, and the strange effects that could be created by moving the original during the scanning process) – which would also inspire the later Copy Art movement.

Photocopying proved essential to Punk culture for a number of reasons: it guaranteed individual freedom of expression, it encouraged a do-it-yourself attitude, and it was cheap and accessible. Furthermore, the freedom to sample and juxtapose images led to the production of collages that enabled the Punk zinester to re-appropriate media in new and liberating ways – techniques which remain in use in various forms to this day. Also, publications such as *Maximumrocknroll's Book Your Own Fuckin' Life* contained extensive lists of contacts, essential for the survival of nomadic Punk bands, once again exploring the concept of building networks within a 'scene' (see also chapter 6.1.2).

More or less simultaneously with this boom of Punk performance-related publishing, another art movement also started producing printed works using mainly photocopies, but from a rather different perspective. The Mail Art movement was grounded in a similar do-it-yourself practice and freedom of expression, suitable to its radical critique of the art world (no curators, no critics, everybody can be an artist, everybody can create an exhibition simply by collecting works by other artists sent through the mail). Mail Art was based on a remarkable yet underestimated infrastructure: the global postal system. As John Held Jr. pointed out: "Bolstered by international treaties, the postal system was one of the only available means of communication between artists separated by divergent political systems."[57]

The first such publication was the famous *New York Correspondence School Weekly Breeder*, a zine from the late 1960s distributed to various Mail Art participants, confirming once again the central role of the 'network' concept. Mail Art zines were by nature meant to be exchanged between participants, in a spirit of 'everybody can be their own editor'. The creative use of this network generated some very original printed products. One memorable strategy was that initiated by the Mail Art zine *Cabaret Voltaire*, edited by Steve Hitchcock in the late 1970s: for issue #3 he sent to a number of Mail artists a 'drawing test', an image consisting of just a few sketchy lines, with instructions encouraging the artist to complete the drawing. The subsequent issue was a collection of the drawings that were sent in, signed with the postal addresses of the respective artists.[58]

Another specific sub-genre within Mail Art zines were the 'assemblies': "The publisher invites contributions and from a few people and each of them sends multiple copies of their work to cover the number of copies in that edition. Each zine copy is then collated and bound making (it) unique, and personalized." (Christopher Becker, writing in *Factsheet Five*[59])

For example, the zine *X Ray* assembled 226 copies of each issue (usually sold out), while the single-sheet *Braincell* brought together donated stickers and stamps, using a cheap multicolour home-publishing technique called Print Gocco.[60] From 1970 to 1982, Richard Kostelanetz's Assembling Press published the annual *Assemblings* featuring "otherwise unpublishable" art and literature: rather than making a selection from submitted material, Kostelanetz (and a few other co-editors) asked contributors to send in 1,000 copies of anything they wished to publish, and then assembled the unpredictable visual and written content into books.[61]

One of the leading Mail Art magazines, *Arte Postale!*, edited by Vittore Baroni, featured theme issues, such as the 'game issue' in which each page was dedicated to a game invented by a different author – in order to play the game, the page had to be cut, folded, or otherwise manipulated, all according to the author's rules, so that 'playing' the magazine also involved disassembling it (and thus somehow destroying it).

The self-awareness of this extensive network (predating the Internet) was sustained by a few publications featuring almost exclusively project announcements, of which *Global Mail* was by far the most relevant. As its publisher Ashley Parker Owens stated: "There's not a single place for the mail art or the networked collaboration. (...) Beyond the projects and exhibitions (...) the true meaning (...) is the exchange between individuals. The secret is in this kind of positive energy."

Another approach to photocopied publication was the one taken by a particular wing of the Autonomist political movement. The 'Creative Autonomism' movement, which flourished in Italy during the 1977 nationwide wave of university student sit-ins, generated almost a hundred different Dadaist and Surrealist-influenced political zines, featuring subversive (often bordering on illegal) content. Some of the most interesting products of this prolific underground scene were the various 'fakes', a specific sub-genre within underground publishing: clever parodies by creative individuals 'hijacking' established (large or small) publications by mimicking their graphic style and typeface. One of the most celebrated was the *Il Male* series of campaigns, which featured outrageous yet somehow plausible journalistic 'scoops', designed to resemble the front pages of major newspapers and displayed near newsstands, regularly triggering a wave of public anger, shock or disbelief.

In Poland as well, a fake of the newspaper *Trybuna Ludu* was produced and distributed during Pope John Paul II (Karol Wojtyla)'s visit to his homeland in 1979, with the banner headline *Government Resigns, Wojtyla Crowned King*. In France, a fake *Le Monde Diplomatique* was anonymously distributed to a number of subscribers, featuring satirical comments on the Rote Armee Fraktion's Stammheim Prison bloodbath.[62] These 'fakers' were all applying in a new way Karl Marx's often-quoted statement that "It is the first duty of the press to undermine the foundations of the existing political system."[63]

Photocopying was also a cheap and easy medium for activist print campaigns, attempting to expand these into an urban territory which was being conceptually remapped starting in the late 1970s. *Bambina*

Precoce, a fanzine edited by Tommaso Tozzi from 1984 to 1986, was posted on walls in the streets of Florence (in the city centre as well as the outskirts), thus exploring an innovative form of distribution. It might also be regarded as a performance in print: one issue was designed as fake street names in A3 format, while another took the form of a tourist-guide map of graffiti to be found in the city.[64]

Finally, it should be mentioned in passing that (at least) two other technologies were used marginally during this same period in order to print zines. Architecture students used a technique called heliography, which produced zines in long scroll-like sheets – somewhat similar to fax zines, which were sent using facsimile (fax) machines. In both these cases, circulation was limited, and copies were transmitted straight to the readers' machines, often through a pyramidal distribution scheme using a small number of 'nodes' and sub-nodes that faxed the zine to a restricted number of readers.

2.7 THE DIGITAL REVOLUTION, AND THE PEAK AND FALL OF ZINES.

But the most important development to revolutionise print was surely the explosion of digital technology. Starting in the late 1980s, anyone could purchase Desktop Publishing (DTP) software in computer shops; from now on, simply owning a personal computer and a printer meant potentially having all the means of production in one's own home. Amateurs (often referred to as the 'bedroom generation') could now produce printed materials in their own personal environment. At the same time, new digital storage media were being introduced, such as the floppy disk, which was cheap and compact and could carry a reasonable amount of data.

Meet the Press, Apple desktop publishing advertisement, 1985

One of the very first periodical publications to make use of computer-related storage media was *Between C & D*, a New York quarterly literary magazine edited by Joel Rose and Catherine Texier and published between 1983 and 1990; contributors included Kathy Acker and Dennis Cooper. The magazine (tagline: "Sex. Drugs. Danger. Violence. Computers.") was printed on computer paper and sold in a plastic bag. The limited-run editions were collected by New York galleries and libraries, while back issues could be purchased on computer disks.[65]

A number of zines started enhancing their printed editions with a floppy disk featuring 'bonus' content. One of the more conceptual applications was created by the Italian literary and Mail Art zine *Adenoidi*, adding a floppy disk containing colour pictures – which were also printed in black-and-white inside the paper zine itself, with the missing colours indicated by text captions with arrows pointing to the corresponding fields. More and more publications were designed as 'interactive' magazines, experimenting with various media such as the emerging CD-ROM. One trend was to reproduce as faithfully as possible the conventions and standards of print, while adding 'bonus' animated or audio content. *Blender* magazine (and its close competitor, *Launch*) was one of the very first to do this, in 1994 – publishing a CD-ROM magazine with original pop music-oriented content, including advertisements.

Launch, commercial for CD-ROM magazine, issue #20, 1998

Various 'interactive' CD-ROM magazines were also produced which focused on experimental interfaces, such as the seminal (and almost impossible to navigate) *Blam!*, which was in fact more a purely digital product than a normal 'publication'. Yet another genre was defined by the emerging profession of digital designers, as exemplified by the mixed-digital-media *Gas Book*, a publication showcasing multimedia and electronic music talents within a single package consisting of a book, a CD-ROM, an audio CD, stickers and a T-shirt.

Probably also as a result of the arrival of digital media, the early

Blam!, experimental
CD-ROM magazine,
issue #3, 1998

1990s saw an unprecedented peak in the production of zines, culminating in the phenomenal *Factsheet Five*, the 'mother of all zines' which for almost twenty years served as "the connecting tissue holding together a mutant media beast" (Gareth Branwyn, *Jamming the Media*[66]). Founded by Mike Gunderloy in 1982 (in 1987, he was also running a zine Bulletin Board System (BBS), one of the first associated with an underground publication), *Factsheet Five* reviewed more than a thousand zines in each issue. By 1990 Gunderloy quit, since he could no longer cope with the huge workload. Eventually Seth Friedman, an active figure in the zine community, stepped up to take his place, and was very successful in dealing with a rapidly growing and increasingly productive international scene.

By the late 1990s, the number of zines had exploded to an estimated 50,000, covering all kinds of social and personal themes. The zine scene featured well-attended meetings, professional distributors and dedicated sections in public libraries. As Gunderloy said in the introduction to his book *The World of Zines*: "The zine world is in fact a network of networks".[67] But the economic crisis of the mid-1990s took its toll on the paper zines: increases in postage rates and bankruptcies of some of the major zine distributors (most notably Desert Moon) forced the zines towards a much more cautious publishing policy.

Furthermore, by the late 1990s the mediascape was — once again — being completely reshaped. Already in 1995, just as the World Wide Web was about to take off, John Markoff wrote in the *New York Times*: "Anyone with a modem is potentially a global pamphleteer."[68] In the first decade of the 21st century, most zines stopped publishing on paper, choosing instead for a web-based platform. This too would soon be superseded by a new (and controversial) phenomenon, the (literally) millions of blogs and the ensuing 'blogosphere' — to mention here in passing a complex and diverse phenomenon which we shall analyse more in depth in chapter 4.

Only science fiction could predict what might come next: and indeed, a fascinating vision of the relationship between paper and pixel was formulated by the science-fiction author William Gibson, an absolute master of twisting today's reality into tomorrow's possibility. His story *Agrippa*, written in 1992, was an electronic poem, sold as an expensive

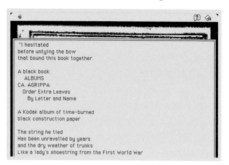

A screenshot from William Gibson's electronic book *Agrippa*, 1992

limited-edition work in a decorated case and with a 3.5" floppy disk containing the entire text. The software was designed to let the user turn the pages on the screen by clicking a computer mouse. But the pages, once turned, were immediately deleted from the disk. Also, the printed book was treated with photosensitive chemicals, so that the words and images gradually faded as the book was exposed to light. So once the book was read, it was gone forever. This work can be understood as a reflection on our faith in paper, as well as a representation of the instability of electrons – and it certainly sheds a light on the uncertain future of publishing in both paper and electronic media, while predicting how the two are destined to become increasingly intertwined.

2.8   INTERTWINING MEDIA, A LOOK AT THE NEAR FUTURE.

"Zines are purely libertarian", declared Stephen Schwartz in his *History of Zines*.[69] This is a definition which can be expanded to include any of the best underground publishing productions. Yet we may ask, does it still hold true in the current digital era? What does it mean to create an 'alternative publication' within this new environment? The basic requirements remain the same: to challenge the prevailing medium, to formulate a new original aesthetic based on the new medium's qualities, and to generate content which is relevant to the contemporary situation. The trailblazing 'intermedia' concept formulated in the mid-1960s by Fluxus artist Dick Higgins seems to have now become the norm; and while independent publishers in the 21st century are increasingly apprehensive about their future survival, they will certainly use offset printing, photocopies, print on demand, PDF files, blogs, or whatever combination of media happens to be most useful for their current project.

On the other hand, while our trust in print remains more or less intact, we increasingly perceive printed media as being too slow in delivering content, compared to the 'live' digital media which can be constantly updated minute-by-minute. This is true especially in the case of the news, which is increasingly seen as being completely 'disembodied'. A clear sign of this is the desperate trend of online platforms attempting to speculate on ongoing news developments, by constantly anticipating what may be going on, or what is about to happen very soon – often using a vague and elusive tone designed to trick the reader into trusting that all the developments mentioned in the news have already actually taken place (see chapter 3.3).

The artwork *Newstweek*[70] (the name is a twist on the well-known *Newsweek* magazine) playfully yet disturbingly challenges our blind trust in easily modifiable online content such as news. Artists Julian Oliver and Danja Vasiliev built a miniature electronic device resembling a laptop charger which, once plugged in, accesses local wireless networks (in a café, for example) and makes it possible for the artists to edit in real time the content shown on other people's internet browsers, including news stories published on the websites of popular newspapers. So an unsuspecting user might find himself suddenly reading outrageous headlines (such as *Milk and Hormones: Why Your Son Has Breasts* or *Thomas Pynchon to Wed Lady Gaga*). One journalist, who personally experienced the effects of the device on one of her articles, had to call the newspaper before realising she was the only one reading the seamlessly modified content.

Flyer of *Newstweek* by Julian Oliver and Danja Vasiliev, 2011

One of the most significant alternative projects of the new millennium was surely the amazing campaign by the activist duo The Yes Men (in collaboration with Steve Lambert and The Anti-Advertising Agency, and anonymously sponsored), which took place in New York City on November 12, 2008.[71] The campaign involved printing and distributing several thousand copies of a fake *New York Times Special Edition* set in the near future (July 4, 2009) and featuring only positive news, perhaps briefly plausible after Barack Obama's election as U.S.

The New York Times

Special Edition
Today, clouds part, more sunshine; recent gloom passes. Tonight, strong leftward winds. Tomorrow, a new day. Weather map throughout.

VOL. CLXIV . . No. 54,631   NEW YORK, SATURDAY, JULY 4, 2009   FREE

Nation Sets Its Sights on Building Sane Economy

True Cost Tax, Salary Caps, Trust-Busting Top List

By T. VEBLEN

The President has called for swift passage of the Safeguards for a Sane Economy (S.A.N.E.) bill. The omnibus economic package includes a federal maximum wage, mandatory "True Cost Accounting," a phased withdrawal from complex financial instruments, and other measures intended to improve life for ordinary Americans. (See highlights box on Page A10.) He also repeated earlier calls for passage of the "Ban on Lobbying" bill currently making its way through Congress.

Treasury Secretary Paul Krugman stressed the importance of the bill. "Markets make great servants, terrible leaders, and absurd religions," said Krugman, quoting Paul Hawken, an advocate of corporate responsibility and author of "Blessed Unrest, How the Largest Movement in the World Came into Being and Why No One Saw It Coming."

"At this point, the market is our leader and our religion. No wonder the median standard of living has been declining so much for so long."

Krugman said that the new Treasury bill seeks to ensure the prosperity of all citizens, rather than simply supporting large corporations and the wealthy. "The market is supposed to serve us. Unfortunately, we have ended up serving the market. That's very bad."

Much as Roosevelt, after the Great Depression, put the brakes on C.E.O. wages and irresponsible banking practices, administration officials claim that today we need to rein in the industry that has caused such chaos and misery.

"The building blocks of post-World War II American middle-class prosperity have all been swept away," said House Speaker Nancy Pelosi, who initially op-

Continued on Page A10

Maximum Wage Law Succeeds

Salary Caps Will Help Stabilize Economy

By J.K. MALONE

WASHINGTON — After long and often bitter debate, Congress has passed legislation, firmly fought for by labor and progressive groups, that will limit top salaries to fifteen times the minimum wage. Tying the bill to a plan of overall reform of the U.S. economy, the bill echoes a similar effort enacted by President Franklin Roosevelt in 1942, which was followed by the longest period of growth for the middle class in U.S. history.

"When C.E.O. salaries remain stable thanks to high taxation of high salaries, there's little incentive to take big risks with shareholders' money, and the economy remains in a steady growth mode," said Senator Barney Frank, one of the bill's cosponsors. "But when C.E.O. salaries can fly through the roof, there's a very strong incentive for C.E.O.s

Continued on Page A10

TREASURY ANNOUNCES "TRUE COST" TAX PLAN

By MARCUS S. DRIGGS

The longawaited "True Cost" plan, which requires product prices to reflect their cost to society, has been signed into law.

Beginning next month, throwaway items like plastic water bottles and other items which are wasteful or damaging to the environment will be heavily taxed, as in many developed countries. Steep taxes will also apply to large cars and gasoline.

The new plan calls for a 200 percent tax on gasoline, comparable to the one long in effect in most European countries. Companies and consumers are already switching to cleaner and more efficient technologies like mass transit and bargain-basement-priced electric cars. "We suddenly have a waiting list 200 names long for the EV1," said Jake Clutter, the owner of Clutter Chevrolet in

Continued on Page A10

IRAQ WAR ENDS

U.S. Army helicopters begin moving troops and equipment from Saddam Hussein's former Baghdad palace.
COURTESY ARMY.MIL

Recruiters Train for New Life

As a ban is imposed on recruiting minors, ex-recruiters nationwide look for new work. The Times follows one on his jobhunt odyssey through Manhattan and surrounding areas.

BY BARRY GLOAD, PAGE A10

USA Patriot Act Repealed

Eight years later, a shamefaced Congress quietly repeals the much-maligned USA Patriot Act, unanimously — or almost.

BY SYBIL LUDINGTON, PAGE A9

Evangelicals Open Homes to Refugees

Up to a million Iraqi exiles — nearly half of the total — will find sanctuary in Christian homes across the U.S., vows the National Association of Evangelicals. Other denominations are expected to follow.

BY W. WILBERFORCE, PAGE A3

Public Relations Industry Starts to Shut Down

The public relations industry has been criticized for misleading the American people, corrupting the political process, and even helping to start wars. Now, it's beginning the process of shutting down for good.

BY LOUIS BECK, PAGE A6

Ex-Secretary Apologizes for W.M.D. Scare

300,000 Troops Never Faced Risk of Instant Obliteration

By FRANK LARRIMORE

Ex-Secretary of State Condoleezza Rice reassured soldiers that the Bush Administration had known well before the invasion that Saddam Hussein lacked weapons of mass destruction.

"Now that all of you brave servicemen and women are returning, it's important to us to reassure you, and the American people, that we were certain Hussein had no W.M.D.s and that he would never launch a first strike against the U.S.," Ms. Rice told a group of wounded soldiers at a Veterans' Administration hospital yesterday.

"I want you to know that if we had had the slightest suspicion that Saddam could use W.M.D.s against you, we never would have sent hundreds of thousands of you to be sitting ducks on the Iraqi border for several months."

Ms. Rice was referring to the fact that by August 2002, eight months before the ground invasion, the US had over 100,000 troops stationed in countries throughout the Gulf, a number that grew to over 200,000 shortly before the 2003 attack on Baghdad. Most of these were within range of the Scud missiles used by Mr. Hussein in the 1991 Gulf War, that could easily have been fitted with chemical or biological weapons if they had existed.

Rice noted that in the 1991 Gulf War, Hussein had used missiles to launch attacks on Israel, which made him popular with Arab citizens throughout the Middle East.

"Do you really think we would have given Saddam a major public relations coup by allowing him to annihilate tens of thousands of you right there on Iraqi territory?" asked Ms. Rice.

Former Secretary of State Henry A. Kissinger responded to Ms. Rice's revelation without surprise. "Of course this was the case. When Israel believed Iraq had other weapons in 1981, they didn't attack on the ground — they bombed from the air. That's a pre-emptive attack. If you believe deterrence will not prevent an attack and that your enemy has W.M.D.s, then the last thing you do is station your troops right next door."

ABC's George Stephanopoulos

Continued on Page A5

Troops to Return Immediately

By JUDE SHINBIN

WASHINGTON — Operation Iraqi Freedom and Operation Enduring Freedom were brought to an unceremonious close today with a quiet announcement by the Department of Defense that troops would be home within weeks.

"This is the best face we can put on the most unfortunate aberration in modern American history," Defense spokesman Kevin Stiss said at a special joint session of Congress. "Today, we can finally enjoy peace — not the peace of the brave, perhaps, but at least peace."

As U.S. and coalition troops withdraw from Iraq and Afghanistan, the United Nations will move in to perform peacekeeping duties and aid in rebuilding. The U.N. will be responsible for keeping the two countries stable: coordinating the rebuilding of hospitals, schools, highways, and other infrastructure; and overseeing upcoming elections.

The Department of the Treasury confirmed that all U.N. dues owed by the U.S. were paid as of this morning, and that moneys previously earmarked for the war would be sent directly to the U.N.'s Iraq Oversight Body.

The president noted that the Iraq War had enrolled in the burning of many bridges. "Yet our history with war affairs runs deep," he said, "and we all know that friends forgive friends for anything. Or nearly." A spokesperson for the French Ministry of Defense confirmed that France would assist the U.S. withdrawal. "The U.S. helped the Soviet Union defeat Hitler. We do recognize that."

In conflict zones worldwide, leaders and rebels pledged peace. (See "In Conflict Zones Worldwide, Peace Moves," on Page A4.)

On Wall Street, reactions were mixed, with the Dow Jones Industrial Average up 84 points, to close at 4,212. While KBR stock was quickly downgraded to a "junk" rating of BBB-, defense contractors such as Lockheed Martin and Northrop Grumman started up.

Continued on Page A5

Nationalized Oil To Fund Climate Change Efforts

By MARION K. HUBBERT

Congress has voted to place ExxonMobil, ChevronTexaco, and other major oil companies under public stewardship, with the bulk of the companies' profits put in a public trust administered by the United Nations, and used for alternative energy research and development in order to solve the global climate crisis.

While unusual, this is not the first time the government has chosen to take control of large corporations. From 1942 to 1944, U.S. car factories were retooled in order to produce tanks for the war effort. And Fannie Mae and Freddie Mac were both created as "government sponsored enterprises" with a significant amount of government oversight.

"We can do what needs to be done," said Senator Charles Schumer, Democrat of New York. "Our planet's survival is at stake. Plus, public pressure hasn't given us much of a choice."

Not everyone felt the move was a good idea. "The climate crisis may or may not be real," declared Senator Kay Bailey Hutchison, Republican of Texas. "I'm an agnostic and I'm staying that way. But see

Continued on Page A5

Popular Pressure Ushers Recent Progressive Tilt

Study Cites Movements for Massive Shift in DC

By SAMUEL FIELDEN

The spate of reform initiatives undertaken by the Administration and both houses of Congress can be attributed directly to grassroots advocacy according to a comprehensive study due out this month.

"In education and health care, most notably, but also in housing, banking, and the environment, we have documented unprecedented responsiveness on the part of political leaders," said Dr. Joyce Wellman, director of the Plains Institute for Policy Analysis, a New Yorkbased think tank. "Our data show a direct correlation between the level of activity of particular coalitions, on the one hand, and specific legislative action, on the other. It's popular pressure that is responsible for the swiftness and scope of legislation emerging from the White House and Congress."

The institute's report shows a three-fold increase in the incidence of letters, phone calls, faxes, and email received by congressional offices. 88 percent of which were from people who identified themselves as new members of particular activist organizations.

The report includes extensive interviews with House and Senate staff, who speak of "unimaginable change," a "dramatic policy shift," and "a new era of accountability" since the elections.

"Not since the Great Depression has the interaction between popular movements and public leaders been so robust," said Jorge Lazaro, head of the U.S. Government Accountability Office. Lazaro cited, in particular, the Wagner Act, also known as the National Labor Relations Act of 1935, which recognized the right of workers to organize and bargain collectively with their employers.

"Roosevelt showed no interest in the Wagner Act until it became clear the unions were going to force it through regardless," Mr. Lazaro noted. "At that point he jumped on it and helped push it into law."

Mr. Lazaro also pointed to the Depression-era organizing of the Farmers' Holiday Association, when farmers refused to sell or bid on crops, blockaded roads, and even once used a noose to halt a train carrying livestock into Iowa. Such direct actions helped push courts and legislatures to adopt

KC/NYC/THE NEW YORK TIMES

Protests organized by Witness Against Torture helped pave the way for the close of the Guantánamo facility.

measures that granted relief from debt caused by low crop prices.

"The similarities between the two periods are remarkable, and the lesson that emerges is simple: if you want change, keep our feet to the fire."

Dr. Wellman agrees. "The only reason the current President and Congress have been able to implement all these changes, was because of pressure from popular

See nytimesse.com for more

movements that made them have to."

The Plains report, due out next month, cites the work of groups associated with United for Peace and Justice, an umbrella for activist groups, for galvanizing public support for ending the war, and for pushing the Administration to resist the oil lobby and other interest groups. It also cites the work

Continued on Page A6

Last to Die

Two proportional monuments — one to the Iraqi dead, 300 feet high, and one to the American dead, 15 feet high — are unveiled in Baghdad, and a five-year-old boy whose lifespan coincided with that of the Iraq War is remembered.

BY J. FERRETANA, PAGE A4

President. The fake special edition copied the 'look and feel' of the real *New York Times* in painstaking detail (including the usual advertisements), and succeeded in fooling a significant portion of the general public who picked up a copy early in the morning (a large network of volunteers, organised through the Internet, distributed the publication on the streets, all apparently without any legal repercussions).

The fact that a newspaper, the most visibly endangered of all contemporary media, was the chosen medium for this campaign demonstrates on one hand the ongoing trust of the public in printed media such as newspapers (as well as our endless appetite for news); on the other hand, the same printed media are also clearly in a process of profound mutation, which is causing a major shift in their relationship with the public. The need to be kept up-to-date, previously catered to by the morning newspapers, is now being serviced through the Web and the even more addictive RSS web feeds, constantly updated from hundreds of sources. And consequently the 'unified' but ever-changing newspaper increasingly aims to fulfil our need to know 'what will happen now', by attempting to announce rather than narrate reality, while continuing to sell the feeling of being part of a community.

The Yes Men's fake but historic *New York Times* sheds a light on the future of publishing: here a 'forecast' content was printed and presented as reality, ironically demonstrating how the 'real' news is increasingly turning into a 'virtual reality': a vast, crowded, ever-changing and immersive space, endlessly navigable in different hyperlinked directions and dimensions.

But in order to understand the impact of this fake print object as a conceptual and activist campaign, we must first understand how our current perception of the news is derived from this virtual news space which we navigate every day. We trust it – because it is printed, and because of the way it is printed. And so the fake *New York Times* is also a perfect illustration of the philosopher Franco 'Bifo' Berardi's statement on the cover of his 1977 *A/Traverso* zine: "false information that produces real events".[72]

Clearly, print is mutating profoundly as a result of its (final?) hybridisation with digital technology – as the last of all traditional media to undergo this process (after music, radio, and TV). And we can assume that this mutation will be neither easy nor straightforward.

CHAPTER 3

The mutation
of paper:
material paper
in immaterial times.

To quote the Slovenian artist Vuk Ćosić (one of the pioneers of net. art), an essential question may well be: *Is a hard copy obsolete?*[73] This was the title of an essay which Ćosić published in the late 1990s on the subject of networked art – a title which itself provocatively questions the human attachment to the tangible, in contrast with the development of various new communication strategies in networked environments. A decade later, we can say with certainty that print has not (yet) become obsolete. But it does seem to be in a period of profound mutation, mainly because of how the electronic screen is already taking over several of the functions of paper. This transitional phase has been predicted ever since the early days of the Web, and was described as being in effect the "Late Age of Print" by Jay David Bolter in his book *Writing Space.*[74]

Whenever it seems that a newer, more powerful technology is about to change the established rules of a system, then that entire system tends to gradually produce a counter-reaction. In the 1940s for example, when the introduction of the first facsimile machine prototypes was sending waves of apprehension throughout the newspaper industry, the Canadian Royal Commission on National Development in the Arts, Letters and Sciences wrote in a report to its members:

> "The vigorous brief of the Canadian Daily Newspapers Association was devoted entirely to a discussion of the consequences to the present newspaper business if the new device of facsimile broadcasting should become, as seems possible, an effective and popular rival to newspapers as we know them... this development will attract newcomers to the newspaper field, and that the facsimile reader will be able in his home to dial any one of several newspapers just as now he tunes his receiving set to radio programmes."[75]

But this time around, the development of networked digital media is happening faster than most observers had predicted.

In 1981 in the San Francisco Bay Area, two newspapers (the *San Francisco Chronicle* and the *San Francisco Examiner*) experimented with making their (text) content available for download by modem, and advertised this new service in full-page ads; of the estimated two to three thousand home-computer users in the Bay Area, more than 500 sent in the coupon requesting more information. Participating users were especially enthusiastic about the possibility of copy-pasting news content. In a KRON-TV news report on this experiment, the reporter Steve Newman imagined the future: "A day will come when we'll get all of our newspapers and magazines by home computers. But that's a few years off." The news anchorwoman concluded: "But it takes over two hours to receive the entire text of a newspaper over the phone, and with an hourly charge of five dollars the new 'tele-paper' would not be much competition for the 20 cents street edition".[76] Which goes to show just how radically the economics of the 'tele-paper' have changed since then (and particularly since the mid-00s).

In February 2007, Arthur Sulzberger Jr., publisher of the *New York Times*, announced: "I really don't know whether we'll be printing the Times in five years, and you know what? I don't care either."[77] This statement was more or less instantly quoted (and endlessly repeated) by online news media platforms of every kind, seeing here a sign from God that their dream of many years was finally materialising. But what Sulzberger was actually saying was that within five years, the *New York Times* would be ready to switch to a digital-only business model.

And yet just one year later, the plummeting of circulation and ads sales, combined with the economic crisis, would force a number of historically significant mid-sized U.S. newspapers (some of which had been publishing for more than a century) to stop printing – in some cases switching to a web-only format. These included the *Seattle Post-Intelligencer*,[78] the *Christian Science Monitor*,[79] the *Capital Times*,[80] the *Ann Arbor News*,[81] the *Rocky Mountain News*,[82] and the *Tucson Citizen*.[83] Others have cut down the number of editions to only a few days each week, or resorted to a free-distribution business model (such as the *Evening*

A street ad about the London *Evening Standard* going free, 2011

Standard in the U.K.[84]) in order to maintain their circulation figures. And a number of iconic world newspapers, such as the *New York Times* and the *San Francisco Chronicle*, are barely surviving, chronically seeking injections of new capital to help them survive beyond their current print-based business model. And the vultures are quickly circling in. Marc Andreessen (founder of Netscape, and now on the board of both EBay and Facebook) publicly assessed the situation in these harsh terms: "You talk to any smart investor who controls any amount of money... There is no value in these stock prices attributable to print anymore at all. It's gone."[85]

According to Jimmy Wales, co-founder and figurehead of Wikipedia: "It isn't that reading is going out of style – quite the opposite. It isn't that people don't care about quality – quite the opposite. The death of the traditional magazine has come about because people are demanding more information, of better quality, and faster."[86] And Philip Meyer, in his book *The Vanishing Newspaper* makes the plausible prediction, based on statistics of newspaper readership in America from the 1960s to the present day, that if the current trend continues, newspaper readership in U.S. will be exactly zero by the first quarter of 2043.[87]

The idea of the newspaper as an 'endangered species' was also the concept of an art exhibition titled *The Last Newspaper*,[88] held at the New Museum in New York in October 2010 and co-curated by Richard Flood and Benjamin Godsill. The exhibition featured artworks which have examined, questioned, and made use of newspapers since the 1960s; here the newspaper comes across as an object and a medium whose aesthetic status seems to belong to some undefined past, rather than to the present.

And what does Google, which enjoys a near-monopoly of the online search market, have to say about the problems currently facing newspapers? Eric Schmidt, Google's CEO, replied in an interview:

> "We have a mechanism that enhances online subscriptions, but part of the reason it doesn't take off is that the culture of the Internet is that information wants to be free... We'd like to help them better monetize their customer base... I wish I had a brilliant idea, but I don't. These little things help, but they don't fundamentally solve the problem."[89]

Meanwhile, Google's current business model of cashing in (through its online services such as Google News) on free news published by other sites, is increasingly being called into question by traditional editors.

Robert Thomson, an editor of the *Wall Street Journal*, indignantly characterised such content aggregators as "parasites or tech tapeworms in the intestines of the Internet".[90] But it's clear that the price of information has dropped. As Clay Shirky, Assistant Arts Professor at New York University's graduate Interactive Telecommunications Program, anticipated in 1995:

> "The price of information has not only gone into free fall in the last few years, it is still in free fall now, it will continue to fall long before it hits bottom, and when it does whole categories of currently lucrative businesses will be either transfigured unrecognizably or completely wiped out, and there is nothing anyone can do about it."[91]

Which is why a brilliant 2009 April Fools' Day announcement, explaining that the highly respected British newspaper, the *Guardian*, had decided to switch entirely to Twitter, could sound even remotely plausible.

Screenshot of the *Guardian's* April Fool's Day article *Twitter switch for Guardian, after 188 years of ink*, 2009

What then can save the newspapers? The German advertising creative director Marc Schwieger shocked an audience at a major newspaper conference by telling them openly that they should concentrate their efforts on becoming the medium that prints "yesterday's news". He also believes that, if the Apple/iTunes paradigm is indeed going to become the new standard, then newspapers can learn a valuable survival lesson from the music industry: how to compensate for the loss of traditional sources of income (CD sales, print circulation) by focusing on 'special' and 'quality' products (in the case of the music industry, live concerts). For printed newspapers, the equivalent of the 'unique experience' of the live concert is probably the thick weekend edition – longer articles and more sophisticated content, focusing less on real-time news and more on analysis, comment and reflection.

The problem of immediate obsolescence (news becomes 'old' as soon as it is printed) is of course nothing new. Interestingly, the very same problem also applies to printed publications dealing with Internet resources, referencing web addresses which may very well be 'dead' by the time the book is published. But for newspapers, this is quickly becoming a flaw of historical proportions, increasingly

Michael Mandiberg,
Old News, 2009

undermining what has been their main role for generations. This shift was eloquently expressed in *Old News*,[92] an art installation by Michael Mandiberg. Every morning, the artist arrived at the gallery space with a stack of (fresh) copies of the *New York Times*, with the words "Old News" cut out by laser in huge letters. The pile of now-unreadable newspapers steadily grew, symbolically demonstrating the worthlessness of stacks of unsold or unread copies.

3.1.1   *The mass slaughter of periodical print.*

Wikipedia founder Jimmy Wales asserts that "There still *is* value in the paper form-factor and there still *is* value in carefully selected 'best of' content, delivered on a per-issue or subscription basis."[93] And what of all the other forms of periodical print? As the saying goes, "if Athens cries, Sparta does not laugh". In the course of 2009, for example, a number of popular glossy magazines such as *PC Magazine*, *Playgirl*, *Arena*, *Vibe*, *Blender*, *Urb* and *Play* published their final issues (though *Playgirl* and *Vibe* have since been resurrected as quarterly or bi-monthly publications).

One rather peculiar phenomenon, apparently restricted to fashion magazines, is the 'digital shoplifting' of copyrighted images. This 'social networking' practice, at one point quite popular in Japan,[94] involves mostly young women taking photos (using their mobile phones in bookshops) of the latest fashion trends in glossy magazines, and sharing the images with their friends through the MMS mobile phone messaging service. The Japanese Magazine Publishers Association (JMPA) condemned the practice as 'information theft', but bookshop owners replied that there was no way their staff could tell the difference between customers taking pictures, and those simply chatting on their phones.

But commercial magazines have already started pursuing different strategies – such as selling digital PDF versions (at about half the
price of the paper editions), distributed through new platforms and
services, of which Zinio is one of the most successful. At first, publishers agreed to give away the PDF files for free, in exchange for personal
data obtained through registration. Later, the services began selling
the magazines, in both downloadable PDF format and web-based
view. An important early characteristic of these services was that they
allowed their customers to share the web-based digital editions with
as many friends as they wished – presumably as a strategy to increase
readership. Needless to say, many people simply shared the cheap PDF
files through their own websites, or made them available on peer-to-
peer networks. Eventually, the commercial digital magazine services
all started restricting access through strictly unshareable web-based or
mobile app-based interfaces.

Left
The historical *Paper or Plastic?* cover of *Factsheet Five*, issue #56, 1995

Right
The Revenge of Print issue (#55) of *Punk Planet*, May & June 2003

Independent magazines are not doing so well either. A prophetic
1995 issue of *Factsheet Five* reminds us of how independent publishers
in all likelihood became concerned about the Web and its consequences for publishing, long before the mainstream industry did. *Factsheet
Five* dedicated this issue to the Web and its impact on the zine world;
the cover story was titled *Paper or Plastic?*, and the front-page illustration depicted a large muscular man with a monitor-shaped face, kicking sand on a skinny man with a magazine-shaped face. The skinny
guy is complaining: "Hey! Quit kicking silicon in our faces, you big
cyberbully!" while his girlfriend is thinking: "Oh, when will Charlie get
online?" The cartoon perfectly illustrates a sense of impending doom
within the traditional zine world, threatened in its very existence by a
younger and stronger 'silicon' bully.

Less than a decade later, the financial viability of the U.S. underground press was dealt a severe blow with the bankruptcy of two of the major zine distributors. One of these, Desert Moon, which once distributed almost 700 zines, finally closed down in 2004.[95] This was followed, quite predictably, by a mass slaughter of independent magazines and small publishing houses, who understood too late the epochal change they were facing. In hindsight, those who were able to survive were those who best understood (and best responded to) the new online media, and who quickly evolved towards a smarter editing model focusing on more sophisticated content. Still, many of the well-established and professionally produced zines which managed to survive the original onslaught (such as *Herbivore* or the famous *Punk Planet*) eventually went out of circulation.

3.2   ATOMISING CONTENT:
        IMPLEMENTING THE APPLE/ITUNES PARADIGM.

Marissa Mayer, Google's vice-president of search products and user experience, stated during a U.S. Senate hearing:

> "The atomic unit of consumption for existing media is almost always disrupted by emerging media. (...) The structure of the Web has caused the atomic unit of consumption for news to migrate from the full newspaper to the individual article. As with music and video, many people still consume physical newspapers in their original full-length format. But with online news, a reader is much more likely to arrive at a single article."

Which is exactly what the Apple/iTunes model has done to the music industry, introducing a new paradigm of selling tracks instead of albums, and thus atomising content instead of gathering it into a greater whole. But buying a magazine or a newspaper means subsidising all of its content developers, whereas atomising its content means dropping the less popular sections – which introduces the risk of an entirely populist editing process.[96]

Nevertheless, this atomising process is consistent with the trend of 'customisation', another buzzword in the marketing of online content. While breaking down the integrity of a single editorial product introduces scalability of content and price, it also means narrowing the audience. When done on a large scale, this also introduces the possibility of profiling readers in order to present them with customised advertisements. Which was precisely the purpose of *Mine*, an experimental service by Time, Inc. (discontinued after 6 issues). *Mine* was a free magazine based on reader preferences, compiled using content selected from the publisher's various titles (*Time, Sports Illustrated, InStyle, Money, Travel+Leisure*, etc) and featuring advertisements fine-tuned to the selected content.[97]

Done on a smaller scale, this atomising process introduces a dangerous trend of paying journalists per article – a cutthroat 'journalist-on-demand' model, entirely focused on the stressful short-term deadlines characteristic of the flow of content on the Web. Another aspect of this cultural shift is that the function of content filter is moved away from the publisher (who would have previously dismissed such an idea by saying: "you're not the publisher, I am") and handed over to the user – which in turn means that the identity of the publisher is altered from being a reference, to being a brand. Thus the 'editorial authority' of established publishers risks becoming merely embodied in a brand name, rather than in sophisticated editorial products.

3.2.1   *Automated content: the news follows the reader.*

The news is everywhere these days: recurring snippets of local, national and world news, constantly being delivered to mobile devices, computers of every size and shape, and (increasingly) on large display screens in public places. Usually this news consists of aggregations of items from a few reliable sources, and broadcast to a large number of recipients. These fragments of interpreted reality are part of an endless flow – disconnected from each other, and lacking context. It's a bit like junk food: consuming too much of it and nothing else will end up dulling our senses, making us gradually lose the ability to appreciate better, more refined flavours. But such a 'bite-and-run' attitude seems an inevitable reality of our hectic modern times.

Echoing the more famous Chatroulette, Daniel Vydra's *New York Times Roulette*[98] is a website which redirects the reader to a random news item published by the *New York Times* within the last 24 hours. Waiting for a news article with unpredictable content caters to the same addiction as waiting for any fresh news item, leaving the news junkie suspended in a limbo of 'what will happen now?' Alternately, the project *News at Seven*[99] has developed a news-generating algorithm which automatically produces journalistic text. The website *StatSheet* has been testing the system using sports statistics; the 'imitation' is considered successful when at least 90 per cent of readers believe the text was created by a human writer.

The Intelligent Information Laboratory of Northwestern University's

McCormick School of Engineering (in collaboration with the Medill School of Journalism) has developed *Stats Monkey*, which generates a news item on a baseball game using "statistical models to figure out what the news is in the story" and "a library of narrative arcs that describe the main dynamics of baseball games".[100] And a company called Narrative Science[101] provides to a few major clients similar software for automatically generating short news reports and updates, mainly for online publishing (and in a way that is apparently devised to obtain higher rankings from Google's search algorithm).

Of course, the presence of non-stop, omnipresent news does not mean that all news is equal. Readers are usually interested in following a small number of ongoing stories. News services cover a wide range of topics, so that there's always something in there for everyone. From December 2009 to February 2010, Google Labs (in collaboration with the *New York Times* and the *Washington Post*) conducted an experiment called *Living Stories*, as part of an ongoing effort to develop a way of presenting news specifically for the online environment. The navigation was designed to make it easy to follow specific news stories, integrating content from different sources and presenting it chronologically and by type of media. The *New York Times* went one step further with its *Shifd* project: participating users had an RFID tracking device implanted in their mobile phone, computer and television, which then followed their reading and watching behaviour. A news story read halfway on the phone, could then be picked up by the computer when the user turned it on; or the TV could be programmed to play related videos. Are the news going to start following us, anticipating our tastes and moods? Certainly, the very nature of the news is becoming increasingly ephemeral – an endless stream of short news items all competing (often desperately) for our attention.

How fleeting news can become a fixed artefact, even a fetish, is the theme (as well as the tangible output) of *News Knitter*,[102] an artwork by Ebru Kurbak and Mahir Mustafa Yavuz featuring software which analyses and filters a 24-hour live news feed, and converts this information into "a unique visual pattern for a knitted sweater". The final output is then executed by an automated knitting machine; each sweater is the artefact of one particular day.

3.3   PREEMPTIVE NEWS:
       THE BATTLE FOR THE ONLINE ATTENTION MARKET.

The news is, of course, a crucial element in the ongoing mutation of periodical publishing. And the atomisation of content is based on a new conception of the news: no longer as the indivisible product of a broader perspective delivered through a periodical publication, but as a single autonomous element of information that can be freely and readily combined with other elements.

MSNBC Breaking News	8/13/08, 9:44 AM -0700	2	msnbc.com - BREAKING NEWS: McDonald's found to breach FDA r
MSNBC Breaking News	8/13/08, 5:49 PM +0100	2	msnbc.com - BREAKING NEWS: Apple September show highly anti
MSNBC Breaking News	8/15/08, 7:07 AM -0500	2	msnbc.com - BREAKING NEWS: McCain Endorses Bush For 3rd Ter
MSNBC Breaking News	8/15/08, 1:28 PM +0100	2	msnbc.com - BREAKING NEWS: Advertisement feature; ŒGuess W
MSNBC Breaking News	8/15/08, 9:03 AM -0400	2	msnbc.com - BREAKING NEWS: Nokia unveils revolutionary new
MSNBC Breaking News	8/15/08, 10:36 AM -0500	2	msnbc.com - BREAKING NEWS: Russia: Forget About Georgia's O
MSNBC Breaking News	8/15/08, 11:38 PM +0800	2	msnbc.com - BREAKING NEWS: Donald Trump missing, feared kid
MSNBC Breaking News	8/15/08, 10:38 AM -0500	2	msnbc.com - BREAKING NEWS: Girl cuts off partner's ear with
MSNBC Breaking News	8/15/08, 1:10 PM -0300	2	msnbc.com - BREAKING NEWS: Girl, 13, wins world chess champ
MSNBC Breaking News	8/15/08, 10:08 PM +0200	2	msnbc.com - BREAKING NEWS: Microsoft's AntiSpyware Tool Rem
MSNBC Breaking News	8/16/08, 6:30 PM +0800	2	msnbc.com - BREAKING NEWS: John Mccain Selects Laura Bush A
MSNBC Breaking News	8/17/08, 12:53 PM +0100	2	msnbc.com - BREAKING NEWS: Paris Hilton Wins Pulitzer Prize
MSNBC Breaking News	8/17/08, 8:53 AM -0300	2	msnbc.com - BREAKING NEWS: [audio] Catholic Church Condemns
adb holstine	8/19/08, 9:53 AM -0300	1	Angelina Jolie's Lips Explode
Aries Lefkovich	8/19/08, 8:14 PM +0100	1	Britney Spears is dating Obama
Neema Roesner	8/19/08, 8:14 PM +0100	1	Britney Spears in training to become lesbian
Armen comstock	8/21/08, 9:17 AM -0300	1	Britney Spears Out of Hospital and Fighting for Palestinian
kenny joyce	8/26/08, 7:21 AM +0000	1	Barack Obama Selects Angelina Jolie as VP

Screenshot of fake breaking news headlines sent as e-mail spam, 2008

Criminal 'phishing' fraud schemes using e-mail spam are often based on grabbing the victim's attention with a fake but plausible news headline. In August 2008, private e-mail accounts around the world were flooded with a new type of spam using such fake news. The message subjects were cleverly formulated in gossip-column style, creating sudden and unexpected new combinations between various celebrities and sensational events, such as: *Barack Obama Selects Angelina Jolie as VP*, *Britney Spears Out of Hospital and Fighting for Palestinian Cause* and *msnbc.com – BREAKING NEWS: [audio] Catholic Church Condemns Metrosexuality*. Such stories, if true, would have fit in perfectly with the other items of any news service – but also with our collective imagination as a whole. And setting aside for a moment the spammers' intentions, the headlines can also be seen as a playful guessing game: who knows what kind of incredible 'breaking news' might happen in the next few hours?[103] While The Yes Men playfully experimented with this kind of news forecasting in their *New York Times Special Edition*, the hard reality is that online newspapers are locked in a constant struggle to be the first to bring the latest news – sometimes stretching reality in order to publish new headlines quickly, and adjusting these later on as more information becomes available. This is what I would call 'preemptive news': information in a transitional state between rumour and actual news, but too important to wait for proper verification, and thus published – as a valuable card in the metaphorical poker game against the online competition.

This 'preemptive news' process was demonstrated quite effectively in *The Quick Brown*,[104] an artwork by Jonathan Puckey, a graphic designer based in Amsterdam. Puckey wrote software which regularly checks the *Fox News* website, taking note of any changes in the

headlines. A text that has been deleted is marked in red strikethrough; black inverted text is used to highlight a text or story that has been added; and red text indicates a story that has been removed from the list of headlines. Antoine Schmitt pursued a similar approach for his artwork *Time Slip*[105] – a 'news ticker' displaying actual news headlines, but in the future tense ("the NASDAQ will drop 4.3 points today"), giving us a sense of seeing into the future, as we sometimes wish we could do – except that in this case, the future in question has already happened.

The transfiguration of information in the digital environment affects in various ways the very nature of publishing. As the Australian theorist Andrew Murphie wrote in his essay *Ghosted Publics*, "publishing is no longer a question of 'readership' but of resonance". And furthermore:

> "Only lazy, old media add up the numbers of individuals who look at what they publish, and leave their audience research at that. More astute contemporary publishing focuses on resonance and the shifting of forces within unacknowledged collectives and

technical networks. The blogger Larval Subjects advises us to think 'about rain drops in a pond', as 'the waves these drops produce converge and diverge with one another producing additional patterns'."[106]

One thing the printed medium by nature cannot be used for (considering for now only the news) is the real-time aggregation, searching and comparing of news stories, performed by networked computers, and viewed on networked screens. A good example of this is Marcus

Screenshot of Marcus Weskamp's Newsmap, 2004

Weskamp's online artwork *Newsmap*,[107] a powerful visual representation of the news mediascape. Using data from Google News, the site's mapping technique divides the screen into columns (topics) in which the size of each article's headline is in direct proportion to its popularity – a visual representation of the viral character of online news, behaving here as a kind of digital life form, which reproduces according to a specific 'survival of the fittest' ecology of access.

Michael Bielicky, Kamila B. Richter and Dirk Reinbold, *Falling Times*, 2007

Another online artwork dealing with these aspects of the online information environment is *Falling Times*[108] by Michael Bielicky, Kamila

B. Richter and Dirk Reinbold, which uses falling pictograms of various sizes, each of which links to a different news story. In this case, the unstoppable flow of (filtered) news stories (each summarised in a headline and a few keywords) must be quickly 'grabbed' (clicked) in order to be read at all. The 'game' of trying to intercept news, relevant to the player's personal interests, but continuously falling in a downpour of content, is revealed here to be an essential aspect of living in a crowded and polluted world of 'infotainment'. Again, the concept of preemptive news, speculating on the public imagination, is an important part of this game.

3.4   SPACE, PHYSICALITY, AND REPEATABILITY OF PRINT.

So does print still make sense, in a society which is by now almost entirely networked as well as screen-based? Print does have a number of unique characteristics which are yet to be superseded by anything else. The first of these characteristics is the way print uses space. The space taken up by printed materials, whether in the shape of document folders, stacks of printed pages on a table, or a library of shelves filled with books, is real and physical. This is entirely different from something existing only on a screen, since it relates directly to our physical space, and to a sensorial perception developed over (at least) thousands of years.

When everything is reduced to the display screen, some kind of 'simulation' of space becomes necessary, since everything now must fit within these few inches. Also, in order to make the simulation understandable and/or realistic, any system for finding one's way ('navigating') within this virtual space should include a consistent interface, allowing for multiple perspectives and levels of viewing. Unfortunately, there has never been a clear standard for implementing this. The different strategies, symbols (icons, pictograms) and navigational structures of various competing systems have not yet succeeded in presenting readers of virtual printed content with a set of standards that they can easily become accustomed to. The result is that a so-called 'clean' virtual reading space remains more unfamiliar than the 'messy' physical one.

Another important characteristic of paper is the 'repeatability' of traditional print. Reading a magazine or a book means being part of a community of customers all reading exactly the same content, so they can all share a single reference. As Marshall McLuhan noted in *Understanding Media*: "Repeatability is the core of the mechanical principle that has dominated our world, especially since the Gutenberg technology. The message of the print and of typography is primarily that of repeatability."[109]

Theoretically, a digital file represents the very essence of repeatability, since it can be endlessly copied from one machine to another. In practice however, the slightest change in the file's content, or even in the technical protocol or features of the machine on which it is being rendered (for example, automatic adjustments or replacements of fonts, margins or colours) are enough to undermine the document's consistency and suddenly turn it into a quite different object.

And finally, a newspaper or magazine can be folded for convenient transport, can be dropped down the stairs without disastrous consequences, can be cut up for clippings, can be re-used for many different purposes. Do all these features suddenly become obsolete, simply because the ethereal nature of the online environment does not include them? Perhaps. But hundreds of years of reading and handling habits can't be discarded just like that.

3.4.1   *The publishing gesture.*

Another intrinsic characteristic of print, besides its tactile quality, is the persistence of its physical presence. The act of leaving documents on a desk physically and visually 'saves' a work in progress. Also, delivering paper documents by hand can become an occasion for social interaction. Such physical properties constitute the unique added value of paper – that which Abigail J. Sellen and Richard H. R. Harper, authors of *The Myth of the Paperless Office* (see chapter 1.7) called its "tangibility factor".[110] And so paper may be seen as a conceptual 'conductor', able to transfer the metaphorical 'energy' it contains, through the gestural act of passing the printed product from one person to the next.

The Dutch art curator Nat Muller wrote on this subject:

> "In this context we view the act of publishing as a gesture that accommodates the political, the artistic, and in some cases, the defiant... A gesture is something preceding the action, and therefore signifies motion and agency of the most expressive and potent kind, precisely because it is so wrought with intentionality."[111]

And George P. Landow noted in his groundbreaking (1994) book *Hyper/Text/Theory* that "movement from the tactile to the digital is the primary fact about the contemporary world".[112] But the more we become surrounded by digital and volatile screen-based content, the more this 'tactility' becomes a vibrant and pleasurable experience – and something that once again physically links individuals, as a kind of temporary neural connection.

Franco 'Bifo' Berardi proposed and tested a possible countermeasure against widespread indifference towards politics, distributing his own magazine about the Italian 'Telestreet' pirate TV movement by handing out copies like political leaflets to potentially suitable recipients. A similar 'gestural practice' was applied by Fran Ilich with his Zapatista-inspired pamphlet *sab0t*, distributed as an easily downloadable PDF file, then locally printed in various Mexican cities and re-distributed in the streets – a physical gesture of distributing the content straight into the hands of the readers.[113]

The attraction of physical print may be considered an 'instinctive' one. The power of paper to trigger such human instincts is the focus of *Pamphlet*,[114] a 2006 computer art installation by Helmut Smits consisting of a laptop, software, and a printer placed at the edge of

The three phases of Helmut Smits' *Pamphlet*, 2006

a window. Visitors can type a message on the laptop, and by pressing 'send', a pamphlet is instantly printed and dropped by the printer from the 10th floor. The falling of the paper, and the resulting 'pamphlet' on the street, symbolise the relatively short distance between personal production and public consumption of a printed product. The installation also shows how the traditional parameters of the printed product have been disrupted: the fallen printed sheet superficially creates the same fascination as a newspaper, making it possible for someone to pick up and read something that was printed very recently. But the personal and arbitrary content of the production (and the almost instantaneous production time) give the final printed product an entirely different value.

And while we're on the subject of gestures, it's worth mentioning an experiment organised by the Dutch *TAG* magazine, designed to take place at public events. Half performance, half 'proof of concept', this experiment consisted of setting up a temporary editorial office to produce an instant, collaborative, open magazine. This performance was first carried out during the 2009 *Transmediale* festival – where it lasted nearly a week, with several visitors contributing to the

Cover of *TAG* magazine print performance during *PRINT/pixel* conference, 2009

process, coordinated by a small number of professional editors and graphic designers. The magazine was then printed using laser printers and stitched together at a nearby tailor's shop. The performance was carried out again during the 2009 *PRINT/pixel* conference in Rotterdam,[115] this time in collaboration with teachers and students of the Willem de Kooning Academy's Minor Programme in Editorial Design. The contributors not only sat in front of computer screens (collecting and restructuring the posts of a committed full-time blogger) but also worked directly with printed paper: passed around by hand, proofread and checked, duplicated and assembled into a single definitive entity to be locally distributed by hand.

It should also be noted that the 'gesture' we have discussed here is not only essential to the traditional distribution of printed products, but also to new collective practices, or 'social networks' directly involved in the free exchange of second-hand books saved from the

Books sealed in envelopes for BookCrossing readers in Leipzig, Germany, 2009

trash. *BookCrossing*,[116] for example, is a significant popular phenomenon, counting more than 700,000 members, who leave books in public spaces and then inform the community of where they can be picked up. Here the 'gesture', and the phenomenon of a reader physically holding a copy, can become a mental connection, which can trigger a wide variety of other gestures in return.

3.5 PRINT ON DEMAND, THE BALANCE OF POWER BETWEEN PAPER AND PIXEL.

Print has specific qualities which remain as of yet undisputed. Holding a printed object in one's own hands, or seeing it on a bookshelf, remains an essential experience in (at least some parts of) our cultural environment. And the 'balance of power' between print and digital (if we still assume the end result to be some kind of printed product) seems now to lie with one technology which, more than any other, is allowing the printed page to survive the 'digitisation of everything': print on demand.

During the late 1990s, most of the 'prepress' services (small businesses which helped customers convert their often messy digital files into plates suitable for offset printing) started mutating into today's digital printing services. Increasingly, digital printing machines were replacing offset printing for short print runs; this was made possible by the rapidly falling prices of high-speed laser printers (the first commercially available laser printer, introduced in 1977, was the Xerox 9700;[117] such machines were originally marketed to large office departments, enabling them to quickly print high-quality structured documents). Within just a few years, dedicated digital book-printing facilities were set up across the world, and the technology is now being seriously considered by publishers, particularly since the onset of the current economic crisis.

Print on demand (POD) is an extremely simple concept: the customer produces a PDF file of a magazine or book, and the POD service charges the customer a fee (there are cheaper and more expensive services, depending on the quantity and quality of services provided) to prepare and adjust the files for the production chain of a high-resolution, large-format, continuous digital copier. The customer can order any number of copies (even a single one) and the product is typically delivered within a week or so.

In addition to the actual printing, the POD firm may offer some important additional services:

1. The firm can arrange to sell the publications online through its own infrastructure, paying the author or publisher monthly percentages on sales.

2. POD firms, especially the major ones, can provide detailed information about their publications to online outlets worldwide, in order to generate orders. This is what Simon

Worthington (founder of *Mute* magazine, which at some point switched to POD) refers to as "the bookspace".

3. POD firms usually operate several facilities on different continents, each printing only for nearby countries, thus saving substantially on shipping costs as well as on CO_2 emissions (and somehow reminiscent of the 1970s, when major international newspapers were wired overseas using large facsimile machines so they could be printed locally the very same day).

4. Publications are not required to generate continuous interest or sales, but may remain in the online catalogue indefinitely at no extra cost, simply waiting to be printed upon request.

5. The cost of producing the first copy is very low, depending on the specific package of services provided to the author or publisher, but can be as little as 10 to 20 euros for a regular book.

The major publishers in this field (Lulu, Lightning Source, Author Solutions) now already carry hundreds of thousands of titles in their ever-expanding catalogues. Amazon, the largest online bookshop, has already set up a subsidiary company called Create Space, as a part of their 'Advantage Program', in order to include authors and publishers "of all sizes" in their platform.[118]

Besides books, and of course photographs, print on demand is also being used for office reports and other business-related publications. The 'Virtual Printer' is a service that allows customers to send a PDF of (for example) an office report, which is then printed and bound in the desired number of copies, and delivered to either a FedEx courier store or the customer's address.[119] Meanwhile, businesses such as Hewlett-Packard claim to be in the process of transforming themselves from a printer company to a printing company, focused on "Print 2.0… that embraces the Web as a channel to make printing more accessible, customizable and less expensive".[120]

There are also independent ventures such as Crowdbooks[121] which publishes photo-books using the Kickstarter model: donating to a project we like, usually getting something back, proportional to the amount of the donation. The publisher offers a preview of a book project, which interested people can fund by buying copies in advance or simply donating money for the publication. If enough funds are generated, the book is published, distributed and promoted.

Finally, one new product that could significantly change the ways books are sold is the Espresso Book Machine, which can quickly print a single copy of any book from a digital PDF file. The machine can process a 300-page book (including cover and glue binding) in a few minutes, which seems to support the American manufacturer's definition of its product as an "ATM for books". It costs 175,000 U.S. dollars, a price which should drop sharply as more units are sold, offering small and independent bookshops an opportunity to remain competitive.[122]

Espresso Book
Machine, 2008

3.5.1 *Vanity press, freedom of expression and self-gratification.*

Print on demand changes one fundamental rule of publishing: it is no longer necessary to invest a (small) starting capital. Anyone can easily raise the nominal charge (typically much less than 100 euros) required to publish a book or magazine. Furthermore, the only technical knowledge required is the ability to properly generate a PDF file (you can also spend a few hundred euros more, and have the POD firm generate it for you). The PDF file is then sent to the POD facility, and within a few days the book is ready and can be instantly offered for sale online.

This opens several possibilities, which have already started to have an impact on various (online) businesses and communities. One of these is 'vanity press' – a term traditionally used to describe a type of publisher whose business model consists of making a profit by publishing books at the author's expense. With the new possibilities of POD, countless new vanity press publishers are now offering their services at bargain-bottom prices.

The vanity press phenomenon is in itself far from new: the March 25, 1893 issue of the *Newark Daily Advocate* newspaper (from Newark, Ohio, USA) featured a series of predictions of what the world might look like after 100 years, by 1993. The journalist Nym Crinkle wrote:

> "Every person of fairly good education and of restless mind writes a book. As a rule, it is a superficial book, but it swells the bulk and it indicated the cerebral unrest that is trying to express itself. We have arrived at a condition in which more books are printed than the world can read."

Furthermore, by 1993 "there will not be so many books printed, but there will be more said. That seems to me to be inevitable."[123] Unfortunately, it seems that we have instead reverted to a situation comparable to 1893, when there was almost no need to limit or filter the production of content.

Clay Shirky, writing on the social and economic effects of Internet, spoke of blogs in terms that may just as well apply to vanity press: "The Gutenberg revolution is over... It's going from a world of 'filter, then publish' ... to 'publish, then filter.'"[124] And this applies even more to POD 'vanity publishing'. The original publishing paradigm, with editors carefully selecting, editing and proofing content before it could be printed, is being superseded by what Shirky defines as "mass amateurization". This in turn is having a significant impact on the more commercial POD efforts, since the self-gratification of seeing a book with one's own name on the cover is an attractive prospect for many potential customers. Meanwhile, the mass media are publicising this development as a social phenomenon, presenting it as some new promised land for would-be writers. This is quite similar to the mirage of what the Internet was supposed to mean for musicians: anyone can publish their work, and who knows, if it turns out to be outstanding (the classic American Dream rhetoric), then you too can become a literary star.[125]

On the other hand, experimental books can now be published without having to spend large sums of money. A nice example is *My Life in Tweets* by James Bridle – a collection of all the author's posts on Twitter during two years, as a sort of intimate travelogue. Here the printed book is an innovative hybrid of something

A copy of James Bridle's *My Life in Tweets*, 2009

momentary (a Twitter post) and something which is meant to remain (a diary) in a perfectly classic graphic format.[126] Perhaps inspired by this book's success, various services appealing to the Twitter microblogger's 'vanity' have cropped up, such as Bookapp's *Tweetbook*[127] which makes it possible to print one's tweets in a standard book format, and *Tweetghetto*[128] which uses the tweets to generate a poster which can then be purchased for display.

An individual's 'virtual identity' (the collection of posts and other activities on social networking sites such as Twitter and Facebook) is by nature ephemeral – unless of course it is printed. And so, as part of a promotional strategy for the French telecommunications company Bouygues Télécom, the DDB Paris ad agency invented a new kind of printed product: an offline copy of a Facebook profile. Participants could order a book of their own profile, covering a specified timeframe and including profiles of up to ten of their friends. The campaign was a huge success: 1,000 books were requested within one hour.[129]

Finally, taking the concept of vanity press to the limit, Fiona Banner's *Book 1 of 1*[130] is a conceptual artwork which "questions the

Fiona Banner,
Book 1 of 1,
2009

currency of the multiple or limited edition". Each of her 'books' is a single-page, single-copy publication "printed on reflective mirror card" and "registered under its own individual title" and ISBN number. Each single copy of the edition is thus an official publication in its own right, meeting all the administrative requirements (which, interestingly, do not include text content). The result is an imaginary printed space, reduced to a single, almost empty page which reflects both (metaphorically) the author's intention and (literally) the reader's face in its mirror cover.

3.5.2   *The frontiers of POD: customisation and open source.*

Of course, print on demand is a medium suitable for all kinds of business models besides vanity press. In fact, several established publishers have started releasing their out-of-print back catalogues in POD. Also, the University of Michigan's Shapiro Library has purchased an Espresso Book Machine specifically for the purpose of printing such titles.

Another possibility, still under development, is to customise the printed content for each individual customer. Various web-to-POD technologies are currently being developed to allow customers to select their own content – which, in the case of books, amounts to individual readers compiling their own publication. Such a level of customisation will undoubtedly signify a major shift in the role of the editor, since it effectively does away with the traditional publishing model of printing thousands of copies of the exact same content. While this obviously means more freedom for the reader, it also introduces a new problem for writers, who can no longer be sure their content is reaching every customer.

Some experiments with this kind of mass customisation have already been conducted in recent years. In June 2004, all 40,000 subscribers of the monthly libertarian magazine *Reason* found on the cover a digitally printed satellite photo of their own neighbourhood – with

Left
Customised issue
of *Reason* magazine, June 2004

Right
Customised issue
of *Wired* magazine,
July 2007

their own location marked by a red circle. The magazine also included several advertisements customised to each particular recipient.[131] A similar approach was further explored by *Wired* magazine for their July 2007 issue; 5,000 subscribers were given the option of receiving their own customised cover of *Wired*, featuring their own photo on the cover. The experiment was sponsored by Xerox and produced using their iGen3 digital printing machine.[132]

Combining print on demand with software to generate potentially infinite permutations of content is already being applied outside the field of experimental self-publishing, in the mainstream publishing business. Already in 2007, the English publishing house Faber & Faber commissioned the designer Karsten Schmidt to participate in the development of a software system for generating complete, print-ready book covers for its new *Faber Finds* back catalogue imprint. The assignment was to create a 'design machine' flexible enough to generate a very large (theoretically infinite) number of unique designs – one for

Karsten Schmidt's generated *Faber & Faber* covers, 2008

each book published in the imprint. The design itself, developed by the Canadian typographer Marian Bantjes, consists of a collection of shapes which are 'parameterised' and broken down into smaller elements, which in turn became micro-templates, thus forming a 'vocabulary' of shapes. The software generates a new cover every second, then judges whether the design is valid or should be discarded.[133]

Software has a long history of producing questionable results – particularly when these results are meant to be passed off as the work of a human. *The Bachelor Machine*,[134] an artwork by Per-Oskar Leu, presents us with a perfect machine-made fake as well as a historical paradox, an "impossible event": "A book signing by Franz Kafka, 85

Per-Oskar Leu, *The Bachelor Machine*, 2009

years after his death. Since none of Kafka's novels were published during his lifetime, this book signing was his first." The signing makes use of "autopen technology and facsimile first editions" of Kafka's famous novel *The Trial*. And the entire process of generating and producing a book, combined with a POD scheme, is incorporated in Peter Bichsel and Martin Fuchs' *Written Images*[135] project: a "generative book that presents programmed images by various artists", all individually calculated immediately before they are printed, making each single book unique and literally unrepeatable.

Finally, Philip M. Parker came up with a rather clever and very original approach to POD. He has generated 200,000 books (which can all be purchased through Amazon, making him "the most published author in the history of the planet"). Each of these books is in fact a compilation of content which can be readily accessed through the Internet. Parker's contribution was to design the software for collecting the (freely available) information (which spans a wide range of genres and subjects – most of the titles are scientific publications) and compiling the results into books (usually around 150 pages thick) which can then be then printed using POD – in effect automating the entire process. He states that "My goal isn't to have the computer write sentences, but to do the repetitive tasks that are too costly to do otherwise." Since there is no investment to be recovered, each book 'breaks even' as soon as the first copy is sold.[136]

Software (which is clearly a defining element of POD) makes it simple to alter the content of a publication at any point during the production process – even between the production of individual copies. And this customisation can go much further than merely adding or deleting bits of content. The POD process actually makes it possible to continuously update the content – thus bringing a defining aspect of online publishing back to the printed medium.

In other words, the latest edition can be continuously kept up-to-date – by its author and publisher, and potentially also by an open community of readers/users/contributors. FLOSS Manuals[137] is a publishing effort founded by the artist Adam Hyde, focusing on free and open-source software (including tools used to create this software) as well as the community which uses these applications and tools. The editing scheme is almost entirely open, so that anyone can contribute to a manual, adding content or helping fix errors, and being credited for their contributions. The FLOSS ('Free/Libre/Open Source Software') paradigm, with its culture of openness, is here brilliantly applied to the field of technical manuals. The constantly updated books can be downloaded for free or purchased as cheap POD editions; alternately, single chapters from any of the manuals can be reassembled at will, and then downloaded or ordered in POD (Hyde has since pushed this concept even further, developing an online platform made entirely of free software for online collaborative authoring and publishing of books, called Booki[138]).

Using FLOSS software for publishing ensures that tools can be collectively developed and shared, and are guaranteed to remain open and unrestricted by patents. The Open Source Publishing consortium (initiated by a few members of the Brussels-based collective Constant)[139] is a major effort in this direction, supporting an organic and systematic use of FLOSS software for publishing. POD is of course the most obvious and natural medium for FLOSS-based publishing. Having open tools which are collectively developed and shared, implicitly guarantees fair access to the means of publishing, thus promoting freedom of expression.

Clearly, POD has the potential to make available in print enormous quantities of otherwise unpublished or forgotten information. POD seems destined to occupy a position very much similar to that of photocopying in the 1980s and 1990s: a chance to print and distribute content cheaply, in a format which is physically stable, easy to use, and pleasant to the senses. Which is still very much what paper is all about.

3.6   INDEPENDENT MAGAZINE STRATEGIES,
        TEAMING UP FOR SUCCESS.

Besides newspapers, the most 'endangered' printed products are surely the magazines. They suffer from a general lack of visibility as well as a lack of sales outlets willing to stock them because of the small profit margins involved. Independent magazines continue to cater to various medium-to-large-sized niche markets, but paradoxically they have become less visible and harder to find, largely as a result of the increased quantity of printed products all competing for our attention. This has given rise to various collective promotional or business strategies, some carefully planned, others more spontaneous.

The biennial 'Colophon' magazine symposium[140] in Luxembourg (one of the largest events of its kind) brings together nearly 700 independent publishers to discuss current matters and to introduce potential advertisers to relevant magazines. The symposium, a sort of collective awareness rite for a very fragmented cultural sector, combines workshops, exhibitions focusing on a number of representative magazines, and the publication of a catalogue surveying almost 2,000 titles.

Bringing magazines together can be a powerful promotional gesture. The Magazine Library in Tokyo[141] is a sort of temporary exhibition of magazines from around the world, organised for a few days in a specific venue such as a club or museum. The magazines manage to draw a large audience by capitalising on their massive collective presence. Visitors can browse the various publications and possibly purchase a subscription to one or more titles which have caught their fancy. Interestingly, the promotional material is usually out of stock before the last day of the exhibition.

This is similar to the business model of Mag Nation,[142] a chain of shops based in Australia and New Zealand which stocks only magazines (and claims to carry nearly 4,000 titles). Here potential customers can read all the magazines for free, before hopefully making a purchase. Additional services include refreshments and snacks as well as free Wi-Fi Internet. The collective presence of so many magazines, and the possibility to read them for free in a pleasant and unhurried environment, creates a situation which ends up generating sales.

Another interesting strategy is that implemented by Steve Watson's Stack Magazines,[143] focusing on a phenomenon he calls "life editing": a selection of hand-picked cultural magazines are distributed to subscribers, with a fixed fee of 3 pounds per copy. Watson claims that the seemingly endless choice of magazines usually presented to potential customers only leaves them bewildered: "it's easy not to see the wood for the trees". Watson says that "life editing is about bridging the gap between what customers like to have and what they spend their time doing". Of course the element of trust is absolutely essential here: "People have to feel that they can trust the selection I'm making." But isn't this exactly what the good-old alternative bookshops had always been doing?

A successful strategy can also be a very minimal one: *Abe's Penny*, created by the sisters Anna and Tess Knoebel,[144] is a "micro-publication" consisting of four postcards per volume, which subscribers receive once every week for a month. Each postcard features an image and a few lines of text; the full set of four postcards constitutes a complete story. (It's worth noting that the name *Abe's Penny* is inspired on the 'penny press' phenomenon: these were early 19th century newspapers sold at minimal prices, making a profit through sheer volume of sales. These publications, which featured extensive coverage of literature and theatre, were also known to maintain rather low standards regarding what was then generally considered to be 'good taste').

Perhaps some day Google will end up absorbing the entire print sector, buying the rights to millions of printed products, selling them to readers through some pay-per-read model, and paying the publishers a small percentage. Until then however, different strategies are being deployed to counteract the steady decline of sales or advertising revenues. For example, the *Amsterdam Weekly*, a free English-language cultural newspaper from Amsterdam, recently launched an imaginative fundraising campaign: each page of the upcoming issue was divided into blocks which were sold to donators, readers, etc, for 5 euros each.[145] Only sold blocks were printed; if not enough blocks were sold, readers would receive a newspaper with blank spaces, devoid of content. This is an emblematic (perhaps even desperate) case of a social call-to-arms intended to support a publisher in dire straits;

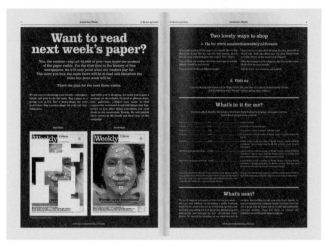

Amsterdam Weekly imaginative fundraising campaign, 2008

yet it also underscores the essential social role of the printed medium, in a way that is quite different from pre-programmed 'social network' schemes. In fact, the former triggers a connection based on shared interests between publisher and reader, while the latter is merely based on a (highly predictable) proximity between 'content providers' and 'six degrees of separation' chains (i.e. everyone knows everyone else in the world through no more than six 'friends of friends') which connect people's abstract profiles based merely on similarities, leaving no room for randomness or complexity.

Returning to the subject of survival strategies: magazines will sometimes cultivate their own particular 'ethic' which can be a very important part of maintaining a viable business. For example, *Bitch*, the most well-known feminist zine, posted a video online in late 2008 in order to raise 40,000 dollars needed to publish the next issue, and ended up quickly raising enough money to print the subsequent one as well.[146]

3.7   THE AUTOMATED DIGITAL PRODUCTION TRAP.

Typographic production was radically transformed in the mid-1980s, thanks to the Apple Macintosh and its first laser PostScript printer. This, combined with various software applications (and later on, with affordable scanners), gave designers and pre-press technicians all the basic tools required to make the definitive switch towards digital production. By now, every single aspect of the offset printing process has been taken over by digital technologies – except the final mechanical step involving the actual printing machine. For example, the halftone simulation of colours and shades, and elimination of unwanted visual noise artefacts (moiré), is increasingly done using a complex digital calculation process known as 'stochastic screening' – something which simply can't be done through an analogue or mechanical process, because of the huge amount of calculations required.

The next obvious 'missing link' towards a frightening (or promising) science-fiction-like 'total automatisation' is of course human creativity. Looking at two software tools that may be seen as prototypes of this 'machine will replace creative people' approach, *N Gen*[147] is the more serious one, defined by its creators as a "rapid prototyping graphic design engine that generates saveable graphic files from the user's own text content filtered through n Gen's Design Modules". The software generates satisfactory, though predictably anonymous, post-modern (mostly 1990s style) layouts, which cannot be distinguished from similar human-generated designs. Though this tool cannot replace designers for anything more than low-complexity jobs, the mere fact of its existence may inspire these designers to broaden their attitude toward producing more innovative combinations of form and content, instead of always sticking to the same old rules.

Another tool worth mentioning is Adrian Ward's *Signwave Auto-Illustrator*,[148] formally described as "a (...) semi-autonomous, generative software artwork and a fully functional vector graphic design application (...)" The author invites users to "discover how easy it is to produce complex designs in an exciting and challenging environment that questions how contemporary software should behave". But the tool in this case actually comes with a healthy dose of irony, often degenerating in unpredictable behaviour and sarcastic error messages, playfully exposing the user's dream of passing the workload on to the machine and the consequent frustration of trying to get it to work properly.

Another milestone in unpredictable digital intervention in printed production is FontFont Beowolf,[149] a PostScript font designed to change the shapes of characters during printing (and a quite extraordinary piece of PostScript language programming). Just as any other PostScript font, it consists of two components: one for screen display, the other for printer rasterising. In this case however, the 'nodes' used to describe the letters are instructed to move around slightly at random. The types released by FontFont feature three levels of randomness, allowing the nodes to move within a small, medium, and large radius, in order to generate unpredictable printed results in the context of a heavily computed, digitally-supported production.

3.8 PRINT AND DIGITAL ARE GETTING MARRIED, AND THAT'S EXACTLY WHERE THE REAL PROBLEMS START.

The business model of traditional periodical print is still based on selling copies as well as advertisements. The free distribution model, on the other hand, though entirely dependent on advertisers, also brings greater flexibility to try out innovative distribution models – including experiments such as combining a free newspaper with a morning coffee, or handing out a free fashion magazine at a fashion store. Nevertheless, the independent press, in its many incarnations, is nowhere near dead. Various digital technologies are being widely deployed in order to support production, sales and visibility.

During the past few decades, print and digital have progressed from flirting, to dating, to being engaged. And now they're finally getting married – which is exactly where the real problems start.

CHAPTER 4

The end of paper: can anything actually replace the printed page?

In 1894 Octave Uzanne and Albert Robida declared in *La fin des livres* (see chapter 1.2): "Books must disappear, or they will ruin us. In the whole world there are eighty to a hundred thousand books published each year, and at a thousand copies each this is more than one hundred million specimens, of which the majority contain only trash and errors."[150] More than a century later, a strikingly similar rhetoric is being used in order to promote electronic books, by discrediting the 'obsolete' printed medium. But can anything ever actually 'kill' the printed page? If so, it will have to comprehensively emulate print's intuitive 'user-friendly' interface; it should also weigh about the same, and enjoy a continuous and seamless connection for downloading new content. That fatal bullet may indeed be on its way – but it's clearly following a slow (and potentially long) trajectory.

One of the loftiest promises of the emerging e-book market, is the amount of space it will end up saving us (see chapter 3.4). In a nutshell, the propaganda mantra suggests that consumers will have more space in which to store more goods – a perfect, endless cycle of consumption. In fact, printed materials are one of the few consumer objects that generally do not expire or become obsolete, meaning they can't be quickly 'consumed' and discarded, but just sit there taking up space, for years or even decades. And so, the magical process of digitisation is supposed to free up all this precious space, which seems to be in such tragically short supply in the Western world.

But will this eventual obsolescence of paper really liberate our shelves of all their printed content? Actually, if we observe what has happened in the case of music, we can see that vinyl records have not been comprehensively discarded; more than three decades after the launch of the compact disc, they are still very much there – and still taking up precious space. In fact, many record shops still have vinyl sections; there are various magazines focusing on 'vinyl culture'; and a substantial number of releases are still (or again) being pressed in limited vinyl editions. Which begs the question: could printed paper some day become the 'vinyl' of publishing?

4.1   ELECTRONIC PAPER,
THE BASIS OF ELECTRONIC PUBLISHING.

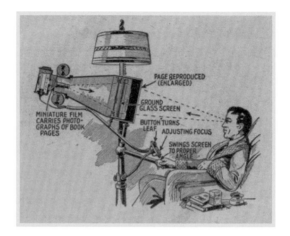

A vision of the book
reader of the future
(from *Everyday Science
and Mechanics*
magazine, 1935)

The first e-book, unsurprisingly, was a product of the usual early hacker spirit. Michael Hart, then a student at the University of Illinois at Urbana-Champaign, used his mainframe computer time (during the night of the Fourth of July, 1971) to retype on a Teletype machine the text from a copy of the U.S. Declaration of Independence which he had been given at a grocery store. He then sent an e-mail to another 100 or so Arpanet users to tell them where they could download the e-text (Hart would eventually go on to found Project Gutenberg, which aims to eventually make available 1 million free e-books[151]).

In the late 1990s, a new technology was announced which was supposed to eventually replace paper: 'electronic paper' or 'e-paper', a display consisting not of illuminated pixels, but of electrically charged

Gyricon electric
paper and
printer, 2000

micro-spheres (or pixels without light) that can be made to turn either black or white according to the polarity of the charge. This technology was first developed at Xerox Corp.'s Palo Alto Research Center (PARC) during the 1970s by Nick Sheridon. The first electronic paper, called Gyricon,[152] was made of polyethylene spheres with negatively charged black plastic on one side and positively charged white plastic on the other; the spheres were embedded in a transparent silicone sheet, with each sphere suspended in a bubble of oil, allowing them to rotate freely, displaying either their black or white side.[153]

After years of producing poorly-designed and cumbersome electronic book readers, the industry in 2008 finally started delivering on its promise of an electronic technology for reading printed content on a mobile device. Though it's too early to tell whether or not this will actually transform the way people read, there are some strong reasons to see how it might: besides the obvious thrill of a new gadget, there's the attraction of all the space that can be saved as well as the ability to access our entire collection of reading materials in the course of our urban nomadic movements ('always available' is another key catchphrase in the marketing of e-books).

In 2008 and 2009 each of the important players in the field (Sony, Amazon, Barnes & Noble) announced and/or launched its own model featuring its own appealing characteristics: a miniature keyboard, a double screen to resemble an open book or magazine,[154] and so on. Besides the product itself, consumers often find themselves involuntarily buying into the associated propaganda (for example, the promise/threat of driving the newspaper industry out of business). The marketing team for Amazon's Kindle e-book reader has already calculated – and loudly proclaimed – that printing and delivering the *New York Times* over a period of a year costs twice as much as sending each subscriber a free Kindle device.[155] Furthermore, if we consider on one hand the massive book-scanning programmes currently being conducted (such as Google Books), and on the other hand the potential availability of almost everything currently being produced in electronic form, then the prospects for the immediate future start to seem very appealing (or tantalising) indeed. But does anyone out there have a truly strategic vision of how best to proceed, in a way that both preserves and enhances all the valuable idiosyncrasies of print?

4.1.1   *The Bezos vision: Kindle the world.*

The most serious effort in producing a e-book reader focusing on the reading experience itself, rather than on a bunch of (arguably useless) IT-centric features, must surely be Amazon's Kindle. This is largely due to the fact that the Kindle was not conceived by a hardware manufacturer, but rather by a giant online retailer of content (still generally perceived to be the world's leading 'virtual' bookshop). At the press launch for the Kindle, Amazon CEO Jeff Bezos declared that "books are the last bastion of analog" – thus implicitly declaring an all-out war on this metaphorical bastion.

Interviewing Bezos for *Newsweek* magazine,[156] the computer-culture journalist and author Steven Levy spiced up his questions with a few of his own remarkable insights, such as: "(the book) is a more reliable storage device than a hard disk drive, and it sports a killer user interface... And, it is instant-on and requires no batteries." Bezos, during

Jeff Bezos on the
cover of *Newsweek*,
November 26, 2007

the aforementioned press launch had stated that, on the contrary, "short-form reading has been digitized, beginning with the early Web. But long-form reading really hasn't." He also boasted: "If you're going to do something like this, you have to be as good as the book in a lot of respects." As far as he was concerned, the Kindle was in fact designed to "project an aura of bookishness".

The Kindle is silent, lightweight (a mere 10 ounces or 290 grammes) and only slightly larger than a standard paperback. The user can change the font size at will (a godsend for older readers). The device can contain a few hundred books, it allows the user to search within the text, and it can navigate the Internet: virtual goods can be purchased through wireless mobile broadband, leading Bezos to claim: "This isn't a device, it's a service." He then went on to describe his vision: "The vision is that you should be able to get any book – not just any book in print, but any book that's ever been in print – on this device in less than a minute."

In his seminal interview with Bezos, Levy also quoted a (somewhat unfortunate) prediction by fiction writer Annie Proulx, who stated in 1994: "Nobody is going to sit down and read a novel on a twitchy little screen. Ever." Bezos understood that the challenge for any reading device will be whether it allows the reader to focus on the words and ideas, rather than on the technology: "The key feature of a book is that it disappears." Of course, he claimed that his Kindle indeed achieves this transcendence of physical medium, and concluded (somewhat triumphantly): "It's so ambitious to take something as highly evolved as the book and improve on it. And maybe even change the way people read." And perhaps he will indeed. As Marshall McLuhan once wrote: "All the new media are art forms which have the power of imposing, like poetry, their own assumptions."[157]

4.1.2   *Resisting the e-book paradigm.*

There are several good reasons why a substantial proportion of readers (and not merely the nostalgic and conservative among them) will continue to resist the e-book paradigm – especially when it comes to accepting e-books as a replacement for 'real' books. First of all, there are the technical limitations of the e-paper technology: not only must e-books be externally illuminated (just like real books) but there is a noticeable delay in turning pages, so that browsing through an e-book is not such a quick and simple process as flipping through the pages of a physical book. And, as novelist Justine Musk noted: how does one get an author to sign an e-book?[158] Of course, the answer is usually: you can't – although in October 2010 President Obama used the touchscreen of an iPad owned by one of his fans to give him an autograph.[159] Furthermore, the typical display resolution is still limited to black and white only. And obviously, just as any other electronic device, e-books are easily damaged by water or by being dropped, and must be regularly recharged in order to be of any use at all.

But there are even more serious concerns, at least for the time being. One of these is that the e-book (and e-magazine) publishing model creates a forced marriage between the user and the publisher, and that once married (once the e-content has been purchased) there's really no simple way to separate. For example, Amazon uses its own proprietary (.AZW) file format for the Kindle, instead of the universal PDF and EPUB standards (native PDF support was added as an extra feature in second-generation Kindle models, while EPUB can only be converted using a free program called KindleGen). And what happens when customers wish to resell or lend their books? Such a simple thing in the real world, but not in the digital one. Green Apple Books has produced a series of humorous web videos[160] about the practical problems of using the Kindle, one of which depicts customers discovering the perils of the 'first sale doctrine' business model: customers are not allowed to resell or lend content which they have bought, a restriction enforced through various DRM (Digital Rights Management) copy protection schemes. Interestingly, publishers brave enough to do without DRM are usually rewarded by a boost in sales; for example O'Reilly, which registered a 104% increase.[161]

Unfortunately, Richard Stallman's radical statement about e-books now sounds rather less pessimistic than it once did: "Using encryption and watermarking systems, publishers hope to connect every copy of a book with a known person, and prevent anyone else from reading it."[162] Worse still (and in case anyone still needs convincing that customer profiling is here to stay), every single e-book or e-magazine purchase is tracked and registered, just like anything else on any network. Exactly what this might mean, was made painfully clear in July 2009. Customers who had previously purchased the George Orwell novels *1984* and *Animal Farm* on their Kindle, one day discovered that the files had simply vanished from their devices without a trace.[163] It turned out that the publisher had reconsidered the desirability of an electronic edition, after which Amazon quietly located and deleted the files from every single Kindle – in effect, taking back the book. Jeff Bezos later apologised for this,[164] but the news (and a host of angry comments) was already all over the blogosphere. Cory Doctorow for example wrote:

> "They gave everybody back their copies and promised they would never do it again – unless they had a court order. I've worked as a bookseller, and no bookseller has ever had to make a promise at the cash register: 'Here's your books. I promise I won't come to your house and take them away again – unless I have a court order.'"[165]

And of course, there is one feature of paper books that no e-book can convey (at least not yet): their smell. The master perfumer Felix Buccellato was once commissioned by the artists Kate Ericson and Mel Ziegler to create a scent based on his personal interpretation of the smell of old books stored at the National Archives in Washington, D.C.[166] Designer Tobias Wong, on the other hand, commercially marketed (in a limited edition of 1,000) his *The Times Of New York candle*,[167] which mimics the aroma of black ink on newsprint; a poetic tribute to the illustrious newspaper (nicknamed the 'Grey Lady') as well as an ironic commentary on the fate of printed media in general. In 2009, the writers of the TV sitcom *The Office*[168] introduced a ficti-

Left
The Times Of New York candle, 2011

Right
Screenshot of 'Smell of Books™' website homepage, 2009

tious product featuring the fragrance of old books. Apparently cashing in on the notion that e-book devices will leave us feeling we've lost something essential, they proudly present 'Smell of Books™'[169] spray cans, to help e-book customers feel more comfortable with their new devices. The product is ironically guaranteed to be "compatible with a wide range of e-reading devices and e-book formats and is 100% DRM-compatible." And addressing a more general concern, "If you've been hesitant to jump on the e-book bandwagon, you're not alone…"

4.1.3   *The iPad paradigm: publishing for the iCustomer.*

"Reading means approaching something that
is just coming into being."
Italo Calvino, *If On a Winter's Night a Traveller*[170]

Apple, it seems, has pulled it off once again. While its iPad is being marketed as "a magical and revolutionary product", a unique multipurpose device, even a complete computer in itself, it is also the cornerstone of Apple's integrated strategy for selling (and buying) digital books and magazines. Clearly, several key factors were considered and carefully planned in order to assure a successful product launch in a new market (as was done previously with the iPod/iTunes combination):

 — A spectacularly designed mobile device (the iPad itself) which can easily contain enough files to host an individual's entire personal collection of digital publications.

- A well-organised online platform for quickly, efficiently and officially selling commercial products (iBookstore/Newsstand), thereby immediately securing the cooperation of all major content providers.

- Locally-run software to handle products purchased online (the same iBooks/iBookstore/Newsstand) as well as digital materials already owned by the user.

- Compliance with existing file standards (PDF when layout is important, EPUB for reflowable text) so that content can be easily accessed, shared and digitised/converted/produced.

- Making digitised materials 'transmittable': the multimedia files are small enough to be transmitted on the Internet within a reasonable amount of time (in the case of print, this has already been the case for several years).

- On the more recent models, the device's screen resolution is nearly indistinguishable from that of printed paper, thus eliminating for the first time another crucial difference between pixel and print.

Using a tablet computer as a medium for reading digital print products is much more than a mere cosmetic enhancement; it is what potentially makes the iPad the next Sony Walkman. Yet the tablet's basic premise is in itself nothing new (a computer roughly the size of a sheet of paper, consisting of only a screen and some kind of interface – before the touchscreen, there was the stylus). Apple itself commissioned a tablet prototype in 1989 from a company called Smart Design; the concept and the design of this prototype is a good example of the computer aesthetics of the period. The device used a solid-state memory card for long-term storage; as Tom Dair (co-founder and president of Smart Design) recalled recently, "we thought that someday, catalogs and magazines would arrive in the (snail) mail in the memory card format for viewing on such a device."[171]

A few years later, in 1992, the Knight Ridder newspaper chain founded the Information Design Lab in Boulder, Colorado, in order to explore the future of news. The journalist and newspaper designer Roger Fidler, who was leading the research lab, believed that the traditional horizontal computer screen was unsuitable for reading newspapers; and so the 'tablet newspaper' (tablet prototypes were currently under development throughout the computer industry) should feature a vertical screen, as well as a completely new interface (thus avoiding any preconceived computer conventions).[172] News would be updated in real time through a wireless connection to the host newspaper and possibly even read out loud by celebrity voices (something which Octave Uzanne and Albert Robida[173] would have been proud of; see chapter 1.2). Peggy Bair, the Information Design Lab's applications manager, declared that "We accept it may be 20 years before as many people

An example of an eye-tracking device, software interface and visualisation used for a newspaper project.

subscribe to an electronic news service as they do to other forms. Already, 60% of newspaper costs are in manufacture and delivery."[174]

So after nearly two decades we now have the iPad, the realisation of a concept incorporating several elements of Fidler's vision. Aside from the embedded platforms (iBooks and whatever else may come in the future) and the predictable multitude of 'clones', this is clearly an attempt by Apple to establish a new category of device (the simplest of computers, specifically designed for accessing media) while supplanting a previously established category (the e-book reader). For the first time, books and magazines are regarded here as completely equivalent to video and music. Meanwhile, the basic physical gestures of reading, which are of course a fundamental part of the 'interface' of printed books and magazines, are being called into question, and thus forced to 'evolve' (for better or worse). In the case of the iPad, the gestures are all virtual – there is no actual physical interaction involved (unless one considers the greasy fingerprints left on the touch screen), but the gestures of turning pages or zooming in and out are very close to the real thing indeed. And having the digital content stored inside such a 'magical' device designed to be used by one single person, makes it more personal than ever before.

The next challenge is not the accurate digital representation of es-tablished printed formats (indeed, this seems by now to be taken for

Knight Ridder's Roger Fidler with a tablet newspaper reader mock-up and video of the prototype, 1993

granted), but the integration of audio and video, and 'extra' content in general, within these traditional formats. Various 'prototypes' are currently being introduced (for example, by the lifestyle magazine *VIV*) in which the traditional layout (pictures and columns of text) is just one of many ways of presenting information, used increasingly as a quiet interlude between exciting animations. The visual power of these clever juxtapositions of still and moving images in a lifestyle magazine is showcased in *VIV*'s own iPad demo video:[175] trendy fast-cutting, computer-generated imagery and spectacular camera work, all build-ing up to the final shot, a classic (static) magazine cover.[176]

Meanwhile, *Sports Illustrated* (a Time, Inc. publication) is pursuing a different approach: integrating videos and picture galleries within the magazine's 'pages' while allowing access to extra 'pop-up' statistics.[177] The magazine then becomes a hybrid object: not a completely new medium, but rather an expanded one. It seems essential that the reader should still somehow feel, and recognise, the experience of reading a magazine, possibly with a few added surprises. New habits are then quickly and easily formed, leading to rapid acceptance of the hybrid. The formats of magazine and newspaper then serve as 'archetypes' for hosting content, based on the broad perception that they have been around forever and still work fine.

Ironically, it is precisely this archetypal acceptance of the 'good old' magazine format which makes it a prime medium for introducing futuristic technologies, which might otherwise meet with suspicion or even resistance – for instance, eye-tracking technologies (implemented using a webcam) that analyse a customer's reading behaviour, and integrate this data into digital publications featuring 'smart text' or 'Text 2.0' content, which is able to respond to the process of being 'physically' read. Apple itself is reported to have already purchased such technology from a Swedish firm.[178]

And so, one likely scenario is that cheap paperbacks, newspapers and other disposable printed products will live on as cheaply priced, self-replicating networked files (featuring enhanced, interactive and connected content) – while physical print, with its tangible material value, will increasingly become a medium for physically preserving valuable content for the future. Which of course leaves open the question of what exactly is valuable and to whom – or how to "find the line in the sand to define when content should be printed or digitized" (Craig Mod, *Books in the Age of the iPad*[179]). But it also represents the struggle between the static and the dynamic, between concentration and fascination, between being absorbed in oneself and being bombarded with outside information. It is, in other words, the struggle between screen and print.

4.1.4 *The turning point: electronic content with the look and feel of print.*

"What has spurred this new wave of hope is the fact that technologies are beginning to look and feel more paper-like."
Abigail J. Sellen and Richard H. R. Harper, *The Myth of the Paperless Office,* 2002[180]

"In the first decades of the Gutenberg revolution, printing presses, as McLuhan long ago pointed out, poured forth a flood of manuscripts in print form. In a similar manner, one can expect that in the first stages of hypertext publishing, printed books will provide both its raw material and much of its stylistics."
George P. Landow, *Hyper/Text/Theory,* 1994[181]

One major (and somewhat unexpected) turning point in the way print-like content is experienced on a screen, is that instead of (re)inventing some new interface (which had been the norm in the 1990s, as well as during at least the first half of the 2000s decade), publishers and software developers started to realise that the original book interface was simply the best one after all.

These have always been two more or less separate worlds: on one hand, web content developers all eager to design their own unique new interface (with catastrophic consequences for usability); on the other hand, graphic designers whose suspicions in dealing with the Web and its inherent graphic instability can best be understood in the context of false claims by the software industry that its products could actually be used to automate print-to-web publishing. Or, to quote a popular joke among graphic designers: "the net was not developed by publishing houses".

Then in the late 2000s, in a remarkable turn of events, the rows of icons and the clumsy animated mechanisms meant to (re)animate the on-screen simulation of paper started to disappear, and the classic paperback interface was resurrected in all its powerful historical simplicity. The most striking example is Wikipedia, where each entry can be formatted into a standard encyclopedia design, generating a single printable PDF file.[182] There's even an advanced option which makes it possible to assemble, preview and print Wikipedia content in a classic 'perfect bound' book style, including automatically generated indexes, tables of contents, etc. The resulting book can be purchased through PediaPress.[183]

This kind of simple, classic appearance can in fact be applied to almost any web page by using an experimental (and free) browser 'bookmarklet' called *Readability*, developed by Arc90.[184] This tool not only discards all advertisements and CSS (web page formatting) trimmings, but effectively strips a web page of all content except its main text, and "re-formats its layout, size, and margins, creating a newspaper or novel-like page for easier text digestion." A somewhat similar software application, *Readefine* by Anirudh Sasikumar,[185] follows a more sophisticated approach, applying a rigorous multi-column newspaper grid layout (while preserving hyperlink functionality) to web pages, RSS feeds, plain text and HTML files. Interestingly, this also happens to be the general look-and-feel of most of the content recently produced for e-book readers.

Traumgedanken, book by Maria Fischer, 2010

Taking the effort to combine print and digital characteristics to its ultimate material conclusion, *Traumgedanken* ('Thoughts on Dreams'), an experimental design book by Maria Fischer,[186] is a "collection of literary, philosophical, psychological and scientific (sic) texts which provide an insight into different dream theories." In the process of writing about dreams, with all their apparently scattered but interconnected elements and possible interpretations, the designer came up with a solution which is very much a physical transposition of the hyperlink: she connected keywords and passages across the book using threads of various colours, creating a unique prototype of a physically interlinked text.

4.1.5 *Newspapers on-screen and off-screen.*

"Electric circuitry does not support the extension of visual modalities
in any degree approaching the visual power of the printed word."
Marshall McLuhan, *The Gutenberg Galaxy*, 1962[187]

The newspaper remains the most familiar, effective and established format for delivering news. In the late 1970s, Sarah Charlesworth produced a series of artworks called *Modern History*,[188] in which she replaced all the columns of text and headlines on the front pages of various newspapers with blank space, leaving only the newspaper logo and the pictures. The result is still instantly recognisable as a newspaper, confirming (and reinforcing) its status as an iconic standard for graphically organising information.

And so it is surely no accident that Google Labs has released (in partnership with a few major newspaper publishers, and sharing with them the revenues generated through context-sensitive ads) a news tool called Google Fast Flip which gives a 'print look' to its very popular Google News service.[189]

Having a literally freshly printed newspaper (or some equivalent, digital or otherwise) has always been a highly valued resource, if not necessarily a luxury. In 1936 in the United States various prototypes of the Newspaper via Radio Facsimile[190] started offering condensed versions of newspapers (a few pages long) sent through radio waves and printed on facsimile paper by a special printer integrated in the radio receiver. The technology was developed to enable distribution of national newspapers to potentially every household across this huge country, something otherwise impossible at the time through traditional methods of printing and distribution. Though the medium was doomed from the start by enormous technical limitations (slowness, poor reproduction of images, small paper sizes), most major newspapers offered a facsimile edition, such as the *New York Times* which published its first four-page facsimile on February 16th, 1948.

It's interesting to note how, in our post-digital era, similar concepts are still being developed: the Little Printer, for example, is (as the name suggests) a cute little printer that can print a set of headlines from news sources and various other content (including personal messages) on a single strip of thermal paper from a mobile device.[191]

For the rapidly growing e-publishing industry, newspapers constitute a key element in the effort to get readers to trust the new devices and platforms. For example, in order to familiarise customers with the experience of reading a newspaper on a screen, Sharp Corporation in 2009 offered Japanese buyers of its Aquos TV sets the possibility to download and view the first five pages of the newspaper *Mainichi Shimbun* on their TV screens, using the remote control to navigate and zoom in and out. The user can even have the TV read the main articles out loud using a speech synthesis function.[192]

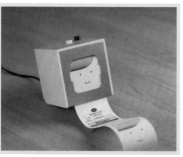

Clockwise from top left

Little Printer prototype by Berg Cloud, 2012

A Japanese newspaper displayed on Aquos TV, 2009

theblogpaper, magazine with texts from blogs, 20 September 2009

Newspaper via Radio Facsimile, *Popular Science* magazine, May 1939.

In the opposite direction (from virtual to print) a wide spectrum of hybrid solutions are available for rendering online news and articles in a newspaper-like format: for example, the barebones *Feed Journal*[193] which collects users' favourite RSS reader flows and presents them in a newsletter form; the more flexible *Page2Pub* technology developed by the Rochester Institute of Technology's Open Publishing Lab; *The Printed Blog*, which collects and prints interesting local content from blogs; and *theblogpaper*[194] which generates a newspaper based on user-generated (and user-rated) news, articles and photographs.

The appeal of these 'take-away' paper products is of course the same as that of newspapers – which are, interestingly, starting to expand their own role and nature by offering downloadable and printable last-minute editions, customised to one key factor: the precise time at which they were updated. Such editions are meant to be read offline, and thus to be consumed at a relatively unhurried pace (in contrast with the hectic, overstretched production schedules characteristic of any news service). All these developments should be understood in the context of a response to a broader need: to bring virtual, real-time online content 'off-screen', into some form of physical existence, as an object to consume and interact with in the real world.

4.2   'REFLOWABILITY':
        MOBILE STYLE IN READING AND WRITING.

Reading text on a small screen has gradually become an accepted practice – especially for the younger generation, for whom it is simply a fact of life. This leads us to another seminal concept in electronic publishing, 'reflowability': optimising the text display for each different device. In other words, publishers (and authors) are forced to surrender at least some (often a great deal of) control regarding the formatting and layout of their content. The writer and designer Craig Mod, in his essay *Books in the Age of the iPad* defined this as "Formless Content".[195]

EPUB (short for 'electronic publication') is the open-source standard for reflowable content, based on the XML and CSS web-design standards.[196] Reflowable content, in its most radical form, has already met with commercial success in recent years in Japan. The ubiquity of mobile phones, combined with the huge number of commuting workers and students, has created a 10-billion-yen market for an entirely new literary genre called 'keitai shousetsu' ('mobile phone novels').[197] In 2007, five of the ten best-selling titles in Japan were 'keitai' novels, including the number one title, *If You* by 'Rin' (who doesn't use her family name when signing a text on her mobile phone). *If You* sold 400,000 (physical) copies after a publisher noticed the success her chapters were having online. Meanwhile, another popular title, *Love Sky* by 'Mika', is reported to have reached a total audience of

The author 'Rin' with her mobile phone and a copy of her novel *If You*, 2008

twenty million readers. Incidentally, these young writers can usually write much faster with their thumbs on a mobile phone than by using a normal computer keyboard.[198]

This is a relatively new phenomenon: the loss (or rather the instability) of formatting and layout, which are sacrificed to the current requirements and specifications of the new digital media. Even the first-generation 'e-zines' were designed with some sort of formatting in mind, including the creative use of the standard ASCII character set in order to insert some rudimentary graphic elements (known as 'ASCII art'). The result was a visually less anonymous product, often enhancing the content within the constraints of such a low-tech format (various examples can be admired in the 'electronic texts archives'[199]). This heritage was also touched upon by Fang-Yu 'Frank' Lin in his artwork *From the Great Beyond*[200] which allows a user to navigate the Internet using a "custom robotic typewriter", resulting in an output of only text and ASCII art.

Will 'reflowability' soon make predefined formatting and layout altogether obsolete? Whatever the case, this is clearly another example of the forced simplification of an old medium by a new (electronic) one. The loss of a predefined layout is not perceived as an actual loss of content, but rather a requirement for rendering the content as 'naked' so that it may later be dynamically 'dressed up' at will – a typical digitisation process. In this case, losing part of the content, its original layout, means making the rest of the content portable, and in the end possibly universal.

4.3   DELIVERING CONTENT,
       FROM DISCS TO WIRELESS NETWORKS.

The early 1990s saw the first serious attempts to create and distribute a popular non-physical magazine – the earliest CD-ROM magazines (see chapter 2.7). The novelty thrill and the charm of the new visual interface soon gave way to a growing disenchantment, which had mostly to do with the medium's most serious shortcoming: its slowness. In a comprehensive 1994 review of the major CD-ROM titles of the period, the magazine *Entertainment Weekly* squarely dismissed the new medium: a (physical) "magazine is disposable, portable, malleable…" whereas "imagine having to wait five seconds before turning each page of *Entertainment Weekly*".[201]

Next came the 'webzines', whose growth would parallel the ever-expanding bandwidth of the Internet. Early webzines were usually organised as repositories of content, often structured following a print-based model of periodically publishing new (digital) 'issues' – while also experimenting with newer formats, which were soon to evolve into what we now know as 'blogs'. Following years of anything-goes technical standards (or lack thereof) for digital publishing, the PDF (Portable Document Format) standard was finally established as the mutual interface format between print and online media. The consequences of PDF for print are somehow similar to the impact of MP3 on music – except that everything is happening much more slowly, since it is extremely time-consuming to scan and convert a printed document, and even more so to convert the resulting series of scanned images into a multi-page layout of pictures and searchable text.

The current mainstream publishing practice of giving away content for free, was anticipated by an underground scene of designers producing a substantial number of free electronic magazines (downloadable or viewable on a web page). These PDF-zines (one of the most popular repositories is called 'PDF mags'[202]) were created to showcase creative skills and emphasise affinities between various groups of designers, and generally to function as a breeding ground for aesthetic experiments and content that was either too controversial or simply of no commercial value for mainstream magazines. It's important to note that these publications are in no way interactive: they do not exploit any characteristic of the electronic medium, besides its possibilities of infinite duplication and distribution. Predictably, the makers of these PDF magazines followed the graphic and production standards of the paper medium, creating a sort of never-born paper product, tossed out for free on online communication channels already overflowing with free content.

But magazines in PDF form also have their own particular markets and forms of distribution. 'Online newsstands' such as Issuu[203] and Mstand[204] use their own rendering software and interface to carry a remarkable number of titles, but without allowing the user to actually download and save any files. Exact Editions[205] on the other hand is clearly designed to sell digital magazine subscriptions, which usually feature access to the entire back-issue catalogue in digital form, as a promotional 'bonus' content to the printed version. And NewspaperDirect combines print on demand with PDF file distribution, offering customised delivery of an impressive selection of commercial newspapers and magazines to specific locations (such as hotels) as well as online access to the same publications (the front page is free, the full content is not).

But once the bull is out of the pen (once the content has been digitised) there's really no way to force it back in. A quick glance through the 'e-books' subcategory on a peer-to-peer BitTorrent tracker website such as The Pirate Bay[206] shows recent issues of major magazines as easily downloadable PDF files. The perfect quality of the files (which could not be achieved by scanning the printed pages) and the instantaneous and regular timing of the upload postings, all seem to suggest that it must be the publishers themselves who are 'leaking' the files – presumably in an effort to increase reader loyalty and circulation, and thus (hopefully) boost advertising revenues. The same strategy can also be used in order to kick-start a new magazine or newspaper: for example, in 2009 perfect PDF copies of the latest issues of the left-wing Italian paper *Il Fatto Quotidiano* were anonymously posted every single day on BitTorrent networks, to be 'illegally' downloaded for free.

The contradiction of having online sales portals often just a few mouse clicks away from websites where the same content can be downloaded for free, was explored (and exploited) in the artwork *Pirates of the Amazon*,[207] by a group of graduate students in media design at the Piet Zwart Institute in Rotterdam (who for obvious reasons decided to remain anonymous). They developed a Firefox browser add-on which inserted a 'download 4 free' button whenever the user visited the Amazon website, linking many of the products available there to corresponding illegal BitTorrent downloads on the Pirate Bay tracker website. One day after the release, Amazon's legal department contacted

Amazon interface after installing the *Pirates of the Amazon* Firefox plug-in, 2008

the creators, demanding they take their tool offline. They immediately complied – but the story had already generated plenty of interesting reactions and debates throughout the media worldwide.

PDF, previously a proprietary format of Adobe Systems Incorporated, was officially released as an open standard on July 1, 2008, and published by the International Organization for

Standardization as ISO 32000-1:2008.[208] Although the PDF format is now widely accepted as the universal standard for publishing (and reading) electronic magazines and books, online businesses wishing to maintain control over their published content tend to use their own proprietary formats (such as Amazon with its Kindle platform). Adobe itself developed (and eventually discontinued) a 'virtual print' version of its popular Flash format called FlashPaper, for converting any printable document into online-ready Flash content, which can then be read as an online book.[209] Meanwhile, the document-sharing website Scribd is promoting its own 'iPaper' format.[210] But does it really make sense to have all these different formats? Perhaps for a paranoid industry (and a few individuals) it does; for the rest of us, it probably does not.

In fact, it seems that the collective 'need' (be it real or fabricated) is now to digitise everything in sight, for better or for worse. But beyond 'going paperless' merely for the sake of going paperless, there is actually an added value here: mainly, having searchable references on-screen.

There are scanners specifically optimised for books, such as Plustek's OpticBook 3600, which makes it easier to obtain a flat image of an opened book using "some kind of 'shadow elimination element' to correct for the distortion and shadow cast by the hump of the book at the spine".[211] There is also software which enables a camera or mobile phone to act as a scanner (such as BookDrive[212] and Qipit[213]); or hardware solutions, such as a cardboard frame called ScanDock[214] that assists in using an iPhone to photographically 'scan' printed materials.

But of course, the fastest solution for digitising printed content is simply to pay someone else to do it. There are a variety of online services, such as 1dollarscan.com which charges 1 U.S. dollar for every 100 pages, and requires the customer to send the original book by post, returning a PDF file with editable text. To speed up the process, the book's spine is cut off, and after scanning the paper is discarded for recycling (though the customer is given the option of reclaiming the book's remains).[215]

Even handwriting (the oldest medium for conveying information using paper) can be converted into digital (ASCII) text using a drawing tablet and handwriting recognition tools,[216] which nowadays are built into all the major computer operating systems: Windows Vista/7, Mac OS X ('Inkwell') and Linux ('CellWriter'). Conversely, a person's handwriting can be transformed into a font for as little as 9 U.S. dollars, using online services such as Fontifier.[217] All of this leads of course to an endless production of digital content, for which there seems to be an equally insatiable appetite. And as designers experiment with every kind of digital medium (such as the limited-edition USB sticks

mimoZine magazine on USB key, 2008

published by *mimoZine*[218]), information is becoming an increasingly cheap and fleeting commodity.

Returning to the subject of newspapers: it seems that instead of us looking for news, the news is increasingly finding us, mainly through online media. In a study by Jure Leskovec, Lars Backstrom and Jon Kleinberg from Cornell and Stanford Universities, titled *Meme-tracking and the Dynamics of the News Cycle*,[219] it was shown that online newspapers post their news about two hours after the blogs do, in an increasingly rapid information environment − which makes designer Scott Walker's digital newsstand prototype seem increasingly relevant (he modified an old newspaper street vending box to deliver every morning the latest (digital) headlines to his living room).[220]

The next step is obviously to have everything delivered in digital format, available anywhere, anytime. The ubiquitous Internet and 3G mobile network (or whatever happens to be the dominant global network) should then guarantee a better distribution (faster and more widespread, yet more personalised) than that of the historical newsstands. This personal and universal (digital) delivery of content previously available only through print, is what might finally convince hyperactive Western consumers to abandon paper altogether, at least for certain applications.

And when sooner or later our overstressed eyes need to take a break, something like *WordFlashReader*[221] may provide some relief, by flashing each word of the text or book in sequence on the screen (while pausing for punctuation)...

4.4   GOING DIGITAL: VANISHING LIBRARIES.

Besides individual customers, an important market segment for e-books is the library. Libraries worldwide are suffering from a chronic lack of space (due to the inevitable physical limits encountered after collecting books and magazines/journals for so many years) combined with budget cuts (due to both the current economic crisis, and a broader trend of questioning the libraries' central role as a repository of cultural heritage). And so 'going digital' seems to offer libraries a way to solve these problems − while also breaking out of their physical boundaries.

In 1928, El Lissitzky described his grand vision for the libraries of the future in his essay *Topography of Typography*: "The printed page transcends space and time. The printed page, the infinity of the book, must be transcended. THE ELECTRO-LIBRARY."[222] The very finite space of libraries on one hand, and the endlessly expanding amount of ideas and evolving thoughts that can be found within their walls on the other hand, have prompted engineers to devise various strategies for circumventing such constraints – powerful new approaches for storing and retrieving knowledge. Furthermore, libraries are meant to be dynamic, to continually acquire new titles,

An article describing 'canned libraries' published in *Inventions*, August 1936

to expand – which brings us back to the perennial problem of space.

The late 1930s saw the development of various innovative technologies combining microphotography (photographic reduction of the original printed pages) with devices for re-enlarging any part of the pages at will. One early 'canned library'[223] was the Optigraph, which displayed pages on an illuminated screen, with a handle for scrolling through the content. The basic concept is strikingly similar to that of the 'bookwheel'[224] invented by the Italian military engineer Agostino Ramelli all the way back in 1588: a simple mechanical device based on a wooden wheel which allowed a reader to access a selection of heavy books with a minimum of movement and effort.

In his 1945 book *The Scholar and the Future of the Research Library*, the publisher and inventor Fremont Rider calculated that the volume of the content of libraries doubled once every sixteen years. He proposed to drastically reduce this volume using microfilm, more specifically his own

A microfilm reader

'Microcard' invention; and indeed by the 1960s the use of microfilm had become a near-universal policy.

In 1959, a *Chicago Sunday Tribune* supplement on futuristic developments titled *'..Closer than we Think!'* envisioned the use of microfilm in private houses, with their content projected on the ceilings of living rooms; eventually "an electronic voice may accompany the

A vision of a future 'electronic home library' (From *Chicago Sunday Tribune*, February 1, 1959, page 10)

visual passage".[225] A few years later, in 1963, Arnold B. Barach, in his book *1975: And the Changes To Come*, imagined the world a bit more than a decade later, describing a system which he called the 'Reference Finder':

> "Every 60 seconds, day and night, approximately 2,000 pages of books, newspapers, or reports are published somewhere in the world; and the output is increasing by leaps and bounds. Libraries will ultimately be forced to use computers such as this for locating documents and references, since it will be so difficult otherwise to keep up with the printed material. This pioneering installation is at the Center for Documentation and Communication Research at Western Reserve University."[226]

But breaking out of the libraries' physical boundaries also means bringing the libraries to those who need them. Based on the concept of the 'bookmobile' (a mobile library in service since 1857 in a circle of eight villages in Cumbria, England[227]), the Internet Bookmobile[228] is an experiment set up by Internet Archive founder Brewster Kahle. Since 2002, the Bookmobile has been physically spreading electronic texts using print-on-demand technology – while gathering widespread public acclaim. Kahle uses simple technology (computer, printer, binding machine) stored inside a van, touring through various U.S. cities and parking outside of schools, parks, museums and farmers' markets.

A few libraries have recently decided to embrace a completely digital model. Boston's Cushing Academy library, for example, spent 500,000 U.S. dollars 'going paperless',[229] getting rid of all its books and purchasing instead flat-screen TVs and laptops, as well as e-book readers by Amazon and Sony. Also, more and more libraries are adopting a 'digital lending' system for their e-books. By 2009, the number of 'digital checkouts' had already grown to more than one million. Paradoxically, most e-book titles are still treated as if they were 'real' books: each title can only be checked out by one customer at a time, while other potential borrowers are put on a waiting list. Two to three weeks after being borrowed, the e-book automatically expires from the reader's account. The software used is usually the popular Adobe Digital Editions. This is all very much in line with the wishes of several major publishing houses (others, such as Macmillan and Simon & Schuster, simply do not allow their e-books to be offered in public libraries).[230]

Still, there seems to be a long way to go before anything can definitely replace paper. In one experiment, 50 Princeton University students were given a free Kindle e-book reader in exchange for their precious feedback. The consensus was that although the device is very portable and lightweight for the amount of content it can carry, it can't be compared to paper when it comes to things like bookmarks, highlights, post-it notes, torn-out pages, and other well-established learning aids.[231]

Libraries, and particularly their traditional physical structure (aisles of shelves filled with sorted books) have also turned out to be an inspiration for artists. Jeff Goldenson's *Stack View*[232] applies the Google Street View model to the world of the library. Goldenson sends book trolleys equipped with cameras through the aisles of various libraries, photographically capturing the browsing experience and then allowing users to remotely 'navigate' the bookshelves.

Finally, libraries are still the place where our collective memory stores the printed relics of its ancient knowledge. If antique books symbolise the way in which we preserve culture, then print-on-demand machines symbolise how we can now produce culture at will (though mostly in poor quality, at least for the time being). These are the underlying themes of the Robotlab group's project *bios [bible]*,[233] an industrial robot that writes out the Bible line-by-line, in high-precision calligraphy on scrolls of paper – thus preserving (somewhat perversely) the 'lost art' of early manual book production, in this case implemented using an advanced robotic 'monk'. But in order to produce such a 'valuable' classic output, even a machine needs a substantial

amount of time: in this case, it takes a full seven months to produce just one complete copy.

4.5   PRINT BECOMES A LIMITED-EDITION OBJECT.

If e-books are indeed going to become increasingly widespread, gradually supplanting traditional print, then printed books may well end up becoming rare – and thus valuable – objects. Art books and 'limited editions' have long embodied this paradigm of value-through-scarcity in print. Such editions deliberately enhance the 'physicality' of each single printed object, by introducing some element impossible to reproduce mechanically, making each copy somehow unique (and thus potentially a collectable object). This strategy has been widely applied in underground networks as well as in the world of top-price artists and wealthy collectors.

One of the most lavish (or kitsch, depending on one's taste) luxury editions to be produced in the era of electronic media was a book on the famous Italian sculptor Antonio Canova, commissioned in 2009 by the Italian Prime Minister Silvio Berlusconi and featuring a 25-kg white Carrara marble cover. This book was a gift for the G8 leaders meeting in Italy, and was valued at 460 euros – though the first copy was valued at more than twice that amount, so that its recipient, the Canadian Prime Minister, was required to donate it to a museum since its value exceeded the limit fixed by Canadian federal law for gifts received by Members of Parliament.[234]

In a similar vein, and clearly operating under the assumption that money shouldn't be a problem, the spectacular fashion magazine

Visionaire produces each new issue using an entirely different format, adapted to the requirements of its content: from innovative techniques in cutting, folding and binding paper of different types and shapes, to an 'electric' issue showcasing 365 artworks – one each day for a year, starting at the moment the 'magazine' is plugged in. A single copy of *Visionaire* costs 250 U.S. dollars.[235] Clearly, the value resides not only in the finished

The various elements of the magazine *Visionaire* 5.7, 2010

product, but also in the 'research and development' costs of the production process.

The designer/illustrator Louise Naunton Morgan has developed a somehow similar concept into a series of print-inspired artworks: *thehumanprinter*.[236] As a counter-measure to the proliferation of machine-made artefacts that surround us every day, Morgan creates hand-painted (one might say hand-printed) originals based on colour halftone dot patterns generated using a computer.

Such efforts to expand (visibly and palpably) the enhanced possibilities of the printed medium clearly demonstrate that, besides merely serving to preserve the 'quintessence' of the Web (see chapter 1.9),

Louise Naunton Morgan,
thehumanprinter,
2008

print can still be used to create something no other medium can – a precious object, something to preserve, to instinctively trust (because we can hold it in our hands), and to unhurriedly enjoy rather than rapidly consume. Which brings us back to the idea of scarcity: if print indeed ends up becoming marginalised by an overwhelming abundance of electronic content, it should still retain some special role, most likely as an (increasingly precious) limited-edition object.

4.5.1. *Intermediate strategies: using digital media for selling print.*

One of the main unsolved dilemmas for writers is finding a digital production and distribution strategy that won't end up putting them out of business. Science-fiction author Cory Doctorow is also an independent literary entrepreneur – a master in developing and showcasing original (and successful) strategies that combine free distribution of digital copies with sales of printed books. His recent short-story collection *With a Little Help* (featuring mostly material previously published in various magazines) was produced experimentally (and independently of traditional publishers) in a variety of formats priced anywhere from 0 to 10,000 U.S. dollars. The book was available for free in various e-book formats: plain text, HTML, PDF (formatted for

Cover of Cory Doctorow's book *With a Little Help*, 2010

two-column printout in portrait orientation) and EPUB. It was also available as an audiobook (again, for free) voiced by professional actors and featuring a new introduction and afterword as 'supplementary material'. Donations were accepted, though not actively solicited.

The book is also available as a print-on-demand trade paperback for 16 dollars through Lulu.com, and furthermore as a premium hardcover edition (for 250 dollars, in a limited print run of 250 copies) designed and produced by book artisans working closely with Doctorow himself, and featuring an embossed cover in comic-book style, an SD memory card containing the complete text in e-book and audiobook versions, and unique end-papers created using paper ephemera. At the very top of the price range was the commission of a new story, for 10,000 dollars, which was immediately purchased by Mark Shuttleworth, the South African tech millionaire behind the Ubuntu Linux project. Doctorow also offered advertising space inside the print-on-demand edition (either "a half-page, or 500 pixels square, or five lines of text") on a time-limited basis ("in month-long increments") after which the ads are removed from the downloads and print templates. Finally, in a fashionable public-private partnership, the author set up a donation programme: librarians, teachers, and generally speaking anyone working in a "worthy" institution, were encouraged to sign up for free copies; "public-spirited readers" could then purchase a copy for anyone on the online donation list.[237]

This multi-layered experimental strategy actually turned out to be financially profitable, paving the way for other authors interested in discovering new publishing and sales strategies. And of course Doctorow is not alone in pioneering this new (and somewhat perilous) frontier of hybrid print/digital possibilities. Another successful author, Paulo Coelho, actively encouraged the free sharing of his books (including *The Alchemist* and *The Witch of Portobello*) through the BitTorrent tracker website The Pirate Bay, uploading the files himself and discussing the experiment on his *Pirate Coelho* blog. The author subsequently enjoyed a huge increase in sales, with *The Alchemist* jumping to #6 on the *New York Times* Best Seller list.[238] And almost simultaneously with Doctorow's experiment, Dan Brown's best-selling novel *The Lost Symbol* (with one million copies sold on its first day) was posted as a high-quality PDF file on peer-to-peer networks just hours after its official release. Peaking at more than 1,000 'seeders' (people sharing the entire file), an unusually high amount for an e-book, the book ended up being downloaded tens of thousands of times.[239] And so the inevitable digital editions and their widespread duplication (resulting, in any case, in increased readership) are already being used as a means to trigger sales of printed books; and the strategy is proving to be quite effective, particularly for established writers.

4.6   POST-DIGITAL PRINT.

In his recent book *Remix*, Lawrence Lessig defined the contemporary role of text: "Text is today's Latin. It is through text that we elites communicate (look at you, reading this book). For the masses, however, most information is gathered through other forms of media: TV, film, music, and music video. These forms of 'writing' are the vernacular of today."[240] Not only are text and print historically and intimately connected, but a text once printed somehow gains an aura of being 'real' and permanent ('scripta manent' as the Romans used to say) even if, in the digital era, everything outside the digital environment is starting to be perceived as outdated or irrelevant – particularly by the younger generation.

A wonderful illustration of this relationship between text and print (and of the 'authority' of the printed word) is *Wordperhect*,[241] created by Tomoko Takahashi — a parody of a word processor, featuring an idiosyncratic hand-drawn interface, a set of functioning but strangely altered tools, and page templates such as *receipt* and *silver paper from a cigarette box* which all somehow 'humanise' the software. This shrinking of the distance between digital tool and physical reality is also one of the themes of Evelien Lohbeck's video *Noteboek*,[242] in which a traditional paper notebook opens up to become a notebook computer (including various peripheral devices such as a printer and a scanner). Lohbeck playfully and surrealistically juxtaposes various meta-medium objects (handwritten notes, software interfaces, digital hardware) to achieve a stunning (yet stunningly simple) digital-inside-the-physical-and-vice-versa conceptual effect.

Our instinctive 'trust' in printed information (including electronic information which has been printed out) was once again put to the test by Tim Devin in 2006 in his *Email Flyer Project*.[243] He printed the final message of a fictional e-mail exchange between a woman named 'Sue' and her now-former boyfriend 'Jay', and distributed the print-out as a flyer on car windshields in six different U.S. cities; soon he was receiving dozens of replies by people who had picked it up. Undoubtedly,

Tim Devin,
Email Flyer Project,
2006

merely 'spamming' out the message electronically would have produced a very different reaction. On another level, the work is also about accidentally encountering a narrative and believing it to be true, since it is filtered (one single message) and printed out, and found on a lonely windshield where paper is usually posted anonymously.

Finally, the MIT Media Lab's Fluid Interfaces Group is

experimenting with a very different kind of e-paper: Marcelo Coelho and Pattie Maes, in collaboration with Joanna Berzowska and Lyndl Hall, are creating what they call "Pulp-Based Computing".[244] This consists of "integrating electrically active inks and fibers during the paper-making process", creating sensors and actuators that behave, look, and feel like paper.

Clearly, traditional print is increasingly being called into question – but is this really a direct consequence of the ongoing development of digital technologies? Or has the digital revolution merely exposed the printed medium's own basic vulnerability? Whatever the case, the future of the traditional print/publishing model (the act of applying ink to cellulose, massively and at some fixed location – as opposed to simply switching the temporary state of some magnetic storage, perhaps halfway across the world) seems more uncertain that ever.

4.7   PRINT AND ONLINE: FRIEND OR FOE?
       CONCEPTUAL DIFFERENCES AND SIMILARITIES
       BETWEEN PRINT AND BLOGS.

There are currently hundreds of thousands of individuals writing and publishing in the 'blogosphere'. From early blogging platforms such as *LiveJournal* (founded in March 1999 by Brad Fitzpatrick) to contemporary content management systems (such as the currently popular *Wordpress*), the blog has imposed a radical turn on the way information is being produced and consumed online, empowering individuals while confronting readers with a massive increase in the amount of potentially interesting information (as well as uninteresting noise). Arguably, the blog platform is already past its peak – at least, as a candidate to supplant traditional news and information platforms, which actually seem to be in a process of regaining the (digital) initiative. Only time will tell.

A blog ('web log') is usually defined as a regularly updated website, mostly produced by one single person, and usually reflecting this person's perspective on a chosen topic or topics. This approach may be traced back to the pre-Internet world of the zines, more specifically the 'perzines' or personal zines. Gareth Branwyn, in his 1997 book *Jamming the Media* offered the following definition: "Personal zines (perzines) shamelessly flaunt their makers. They detail the lives of their publishers through intimate stories, anecdotes, comics, photos, and pieces about them written by others. A perzine is like an elaborate letter from a friend (that you happen not to know)."[245] The perzines remained a marginal segment of the zine world, with a few exceptions such as Pete Jordan's iconic and autobiographically-titled *Dishwasher*,[246] which resonated and connected with a sizeable community of colleagues throughout the U.S. – all touring the country and sharing tips and tricks about their otherwise unexciting work. His fame soon spread well beyond this circle of colleagues, eventually culminating in a book about his life.

A few important similarities and differences between blogs and (nonfiction) print:

Production

– Blogs have low production costs and can be read for free. They usually have one editor (who is the writer, or one of the writers, of the blog) or a very small number of editors. Distribution is cheap (through Internet hosting) – distribution costs are directly proportional to the blog's popularity. Published content can always be altered or corrected later on.

– Print has high production costs, must usually be paid for in order to be read (an exception is free newspapers or other publications whose business model depends entirely on advertisement rather than sales). It usually requires professional editors and often contributors. Distribution is paid for by the publisher. The content once printed cannot be changed.

Access

– The availability of blogs depends on access to the Internet and to electricity. Blogs are searchable.
– Print is always available, but not searchable.

Aesthetics

– Blogs, like most other screen-based content, are mostly read on a backlit medium. They usually aim for a tone of inspired spontaneity. The graphic appearance of previously published content can be entirely (and almost instantaneously) changed anytime after publication. Blogs involve only the sense of sight, and perhaps also to some degree hearing (starting with the mouse clicks), and usually consist of short texts and possibly reader comments.
– Print is externally illuminated. It usually aims for a more thoughtful and less spontaneous tone. Its content is fixed forever in its original graphic design. Print involves sight, touch, smell, and hearing, and printed texts are usually longer than those posted online.

Functionality

– Blogs are published according to a 'real-time' production model, more or less instantaneously, as soon as they have been written. They are usually not published according to a fixed schedule, but whenever they happen to be updated; being updated actively and frequently tends to increase the blog's reputation. Blogs are usually not meant to be printed. One can quickly and easily find out who has referred to a particular blog online.

– Print is never a 'real-time' production – the very nature of the printing process requires at least a minimal production period. Print usually refers to events that took place within a certain range of time before publication. It is usually published according to a schedule (which may also be flexible). If needed, a printed publication could conceivably be converted into a blog format. Finding out where any given text has been referred to in another printed publication can be extremely time-consuming (if not impossible).

As mentioned above, paper involves most of our senses, mainly sight, touch, and smell. Touch tells us something about the type of information we're reading as we turn the pages: rough for plain text books or photocopies, smooth for magazines or illustrated books. The smell of the paper can tell us how old the information is: inky for recently printed texts, mouldy or dusty for older ones. The colour of the pages also gives us an indication of their age: yellowed paper is visibly old (though this degenerative process may take several decades). Electronic visual media, on the other hand, are perceived exclusively through the sense of sight. Only the particular technology employed can help us guess the age (and perhaps also to some degree the nature) of the information: for example, the resolution and colour depth (i.e. number of colours) of digital images, or more generally the influence of technological limitations on the graphic design.

Another essential consideration is the extent to which we can use our photographic memory to retrieve information. Photographic memory of a printed paper object is straightforward as well as static: we can remember the layout of a specific page in a magazine, as well as the physical space (such as a particular bookshelf) where we stored the magazine – and we can connect these memories to other memories from the same period.

But photographic memory doesn't work well with a display screen, which is dynamic, in a state of constant change. More importantly, the screen itself remains the same physical space – only its content changes. When attempting to remember where we saw some particular screen content, we might refer to its URL web address or to a hyperlink that brought us there; but unless we have somehow saved this information, there's not much more that we can do to help ourselves remember. Another important consideration is the lighting. In most electronic media, the screen is backlit. Marshall McLuhan speculated (rather appropriately, during a TV interview) that this characteristic in particular induces a near-mystical reverence in the spectator, much like that of the stained glass windows of medieval churches. Also, the backlit screen shines directly on the retina, strongly stimulating the sense of sight. Paper, on the other hand, is indirectly illuminated by the natural lighting of the environment, and is thus much less strenuous on the eyesight.

Returning to the subject of blogs, a few particular cases stand out, and among these the story of *Boing Boing* is truly unique. Originally *Boing Boing* was a printed zine, founded by Mark Frauenfelder and his girlfriend Carla Sinclair in 1988. The zine was quite successful in the U.S. and abroad, but was hit hard by the early 1990s bankruptcy of the big independent zine distributors, and eventually stopped publishing in printed form. In the meantime Frauenfelder had been hired as an associate editor of *Wired* magazine: he was with the magazine from its very beginning, and was closely involved with its first experimental online presence, called *Hot Wired*.

In 1995 he revived *Boing Boing* in a new online incarnation, pioneering many of the defining features of what would soon be known as blogging. The online *Boing Boing* was hugely popular, ranked among the 2500 most visited websites worldwide.[247] Frauenfelder's career then led him back to print, founding *Make*, a (paper) magazine focusing on DIY (do-it-yourself) and DIWO (do-it-with-others) projects such as building tools and machines, and modifying electronic hardware – an excellent example of how a printed publication can become an important resource for an active online community. Frauenfelder remains a blog contributor and editor for *Boing Boing*, and seems to thrive in this ongoing duality between print and pixel, which constantly evolves along with the technological possibilities of publishing.

But the relationship between bloggers and print technologies is not always such a harmonious one. The queen of art blogs, Régine Debatty (editor of *we-make-money-not-art.com*), while declaring herself a heartfelt and passionate fan of print, also admits to feeling intimidated by the medium's immutability. Debatty is the archetypal independent blogger/editor, headlining her own internationally acclaimed online publishing platform (which she manages with a high degree of professional and artistic integrity, as well as a distinct personal style). Her own popular (and excellently written) daily posts are but the most visible part of an intricate process involving a vast personal network, and seamlessly integrating various newer and older media.[248]

In all likelihood, the nature of the blog has forced a fundamental and historic evolution of the publishing process (and even the writing process): these have become dynamic activities, shaped by an ongoing interactive dialogue between authors, editors and readers – whether directly (through reader comments) or indirectly (through private e-mail). But, as

Régine Debatty, editor of the blog
we-make-money-not-art.com

with every evolution, while something had been gained, something else has been lost: penmanship, little doodles, quick notes, obscure or purely decorative marks, all of which contribute to deciphering the 'mood' of what was scribbled on paper. We have gained, instead, accuracy and heterogeneity, thanks to online (or offline) dictionary software. There is also another radical change to consider, which can be read between the lines: publishing on paper, compared to publishing online, is a stronger 'gesture', one which creates the sense of an intimate (and definitely physical) space between the writer and reader.

4.8   WHICH IS MORE ENVIRONMENTALLY FRIENDLY:
PRINT OR DIGITAL?

Environmental concerns have always been an important issue, at least for the more conscientious individuals and organisations operating within the digital realm. In the early 1990s, when e-mail first started being used on a massive scale for personal communication, e-mail messages often featured catchphrases such as: "No trees were harmed in the sending of this message". Similarly, early e-zines regularly stated that "No trees were harmed in the creation of this magazine", and there are still plenty of web pages claiming (rather mystifyingly) that "No electrons were harmed in making this webpage". The O'Reilly publishing house currently uses the slogan "save a tree, go digital" to incite customers to buy digital editions, while Press Display, an online shop for e-magazines, proclaims in banner-headline letters: "No recycling required".

But is digital technology actually helping publishers to reduce their carbon footprint? It seems the increased amount of printable content actually (perhaps even predictably) causes more pages to be printed. Paul Smith, a lab researcher at Xerox, said that "our studies were showing us that 45 per cent of all office printing is for 'one-time use', like reading an e-mail." Smith is part of a project team currently developing an experimental printing technology: self-erasing, reusable paper which selectively changes colour when it absorbs certain wavelengths of light, and then gradually turns blank again. In its current version, the paper self-erases after about 16-24 hours and can be re-used again and again. The technology, which is not expected to become available for a few more years, is said to reduce the amount of energy required to print a single page from over 200 kJ to just 1 kJ. The paper itself is expected to cost the same as regular paper.[249]

The artist Nathalie Jeremijenko wished to stigmatise the careless use of paper in the office: her artwork *Stump*[250] is a printer queue software virus that counts the number of pages used by the printer. When the equivalent of a whole tree has been consumed, the software automatically prints out a "slice of tree". Collecting these print-outs and stacking them up into a growing 'stump' creates a tangible representation of the patch of forest consumed by the printer and its user.

One slang expression for 'going to print' is 'from online to dead tree' – which is something of a gross generalisation, since the environmental impact of 'staying online' is far from negligible, as we shall see further on in this section. Whatever the case, in December 2010 the international non-governmental organisation WWF (World Wide Fund For Nature) launched a new WWF file format – nearly identical to the popular PDF format except for one interesting catch: the file cannot be printed. Meant as a symbolic act of resistance to unnecessary printing, the format is perfectly readable on display screens and integrates seamlessly with all popular operating systems.[251]

There are also subtler ways to approach the problem, such as the open-source *Ecofont*[252] which essentially inserts tiny gaps in the typeface, saving a substantial amount of toner without compromising readability. *Pencil Printer*,[253] a concept design by Hoyoung Lee, Seunghwa Jeong and Jin-young Yoon introduces a printer that uses actual pencils to print out documents, which can then be corrected (or even completely erased, thus recycled) using a common pencil eraser. And there are even printed products that incorporate organic materials, such as Recycled Ideas' *Herb Seed* or 'plantable paper' greeting cards, which are filled with seeds,[254] or Inhabitat's laser-cut leaves as business cards.[255]

Despite all these practices and their underlying assumptions, it's not quite clear whether digital media are actually succeeding in producing a smaller carbon footprint than print. For example, anyone advocating the use of 'electronic form reports' to replace printed reports should include in their carbon footprint calculation not only the amount of paper saved, but also the amount of electrical consumption required to keep the servers permanently online: "Jonathan Koomey of Lawrence Berkeley National Laboratory in California has calculated that the data centres that drive the internet already consume one per cent of global electricity capacity, and that their consumption is growing at seventeen per cent per year."[256] Clearly, the longer we spend looking at any given information (and the more complex the information), the greater the advantages of paper and print. Barney Cox, writing in *Eye* magazine, went even further, proposing a 'Slow Information' movement (echoing the 'Slow Food' one), better for our eyes as well as for our planet.[257]

4.9   PAPER IS FLESH. SCREEN IS METAL.

The duality (whether mutually exclusive or complementary) between paper and screen can be summarised in a cyberpunk metaphor: paper is flesh, screen is metal. What we're dealing with here is a transitional medium, with constantly mutating hybrid characteristics. Paper and pixel complement each other, even as they compete with one another. They need each other to survive, though they both may have good reasons for 'feeling superior' to the other. Digital media relies on the long experience of print in the fields of layout and content management. And print has much to gain from digital media's atomisation of content, with its endless possibilities of indexing and searching. Flesh and metal will thus merge as in a cyberpunk film, hopefully spawning useful new models for carrying and spreading unprecedented amounts of information and culture.

CHAPTER 5

Distributed archives: paper content from the past, paper content for the future.

"All forms of knowledge achieved stability and permanence,
not because paper was more durable than papyrus but simply
because there were many copies."

James Gleick, *The Information: A History, a Theory, a Flood*, 2011[258]

The Internet (not unlike a human being) is particularly fond of its own historical period; it is much less interested in anything that took place before its own birth. Online, one can easily find news, documents, historical information and other cultural artefacts produced since the mid-1990s, but the farther one goes back in time before that, the less information there is to be found. The sense of history on the Web is rather like the flow of a river: always looking ahead to some promised estuary, rather than remembering when and where its own waters originated – let alone what might have happened before that. And so, even though the late 1990s and 2000s are well covered online, beyond that there's a tangible historical vacuum, which becomes evident the moment one wishes to seriously research anything less familiar than the obvious 'cultural classics'.

The 'online giants' (Google, Amazon, Microsoft, etc) are of course well aware of this cultural gap. They also realise that, in order to firmly establish the Internet's reputation as a trusted and universal medium, traditional media will have to be incorporated within the on-line structure, which means allowing people to access that which they have always trusted the most: printed materials. But digitising large quantities of print is an enormous task, and so there are massive efforts underway for archiving printed content and making it available online. Perhaps this is indeed the final phase of the passage from the printed to the digital form; or perhaps the question should really be: can such a process be properly described as 'archiving' in the first place?

5.1   THE 'ONLINE GIANTS' AND THEIR APPROACH
        TO 'ARCHIVING' PRINTED MATERIALS.

These two conceptual elements (on one hand the chronological bias of the Web, and on the other hand the online 'archiving' of previously unavailable printed content, making it indexable and searchable) have inspired the aforementioned 'online giants' to look upon the heritage of printed knowledge as a potentially valuable resource: one that could be transformed from another (yet) uncharted online territory, into a new major source of income and market share.

Amazon, for example, has used online archiving to boost and expand its core business: selling books. It has done this by asking publishers to 'consign' to Amazon the content of their books in digital form, so that Amazon in turn can allow potential customers to search the text. This 'Search Inside the Book' feature, introduced in late 2003, has since proven to be a 'killer application' for the marketing and selling of books. It is also being used extensively by researchers and academics worldwide. The feature allows potential customers to search a book's entire text, generating search results in a Google-like interface, including details on where exactly the search term occurs in the book: the page number and the text immediately preceding and following the search term (in other words, its context). Access to the text is carefully guarded and limited, never giving a substantial part of it away, but rather allowing the customer to sample just enough of it to get a better idea of its contents. In the end, this method turns out to be even more enlightening (and enticing) than simply flipping through the book in a bookshop, eventually reinforcing the need to buy and own the book.

Such an advertising model of 'extreme teasing' operates on the very thin boundary between giving customers an illusion of accessing the whole content for free, and getting them to actually purchase and own the book. This is a key concept in the transition from printed text to its digital form, and especially the public perception of how desirable such a transition really is. As James Rifkin wrote in his book *The age of access*: "The physical container becomes secondary to the unique services contained in it... Books and journals on library shelves are giving precedence to access to services via the Internet."[259] While Amazon is busy extracting 'teasing' content from books it wishes to sell, other 'online giants' are more preoccupied with gathering vast amounts of valuable and 'new' content in order to attract users (and to keep them coming back for more), in much the same way as the manufacturing industry is fuelled by the endless need to create new products or new versions of existing products. Likewise, online platforms are locked in an endless competition for market share, in order to attract more advertisers and sell more advertising space.

The supreme example of this paradigm is of course Google, with its text advertisements on every search page. Google's strategy regarding printed materials is to incorporate previously printed content

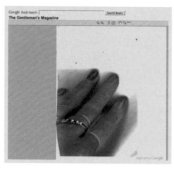

A female hand, probably turning pages, scanned by accident and found in a Google Books file, 2008

within its own products (such as Google Books and Google News). Both these efforts were realised through huge investments, calculated to dominate their respective markets from the moment they were launched (as is usually the case with any Google service). After four years of work (most books are scanned using specialised scanning devices at a rate of 1,000 pages per hour), with an initial investment of five million U.S. dollars and in collaboration with no less than 20,000 publishing partners (including several major libraries), Google Books claimed by 2010 to have scanned 10 million books, with 1 million of these available in their full version. And Google continues to announce and develop new ventures and partnerships, such as the digital archiving of another 1 million public-domain books from the Italian national libraries of Rome and Florence.

In 2008 Google also purchased twenty million digitised historical newspaper pages from a Canadian company, PaperofRecord.com.[260] And as if that weren't enough, Google is also seeking to gain control of the rights to books known as 'orphan works' which have essentially been abandoned by their authors and publishers (though such titles are still under copyright, the copyright holders are either unknown or cannot be found). But when a book featured in Google Books is still protected by copyright, the impression (made by the cover and the bibliographic data) of accessing an 'archive' soon turns out to be quite illusory: as soon as the user attempts to read further within any particular book, most of the content turns out to be unavailable ("not shown in this preview"). Nevertheless, these projects will probably end up reinforcing the general impression of Google as a 'force for good', preserving valuable resources for the benefit of humanity (as it previously did in retrieving and archiving the complete historical Usenet newsgroups). And of course, doing so in the field of printed publishing will certainly bestow upon Google more prestige and cultural authority than ever before, further cementing its position as the 'universal database' and first point of reference. In the end, this centralised collection of news and culture produced over several generations will be searchable through Google's proprietary interface. Content which is globally relevant will be globally sold (through advertisements), yet centrally managed and controlled.

But we're not yet used to searching such an enormous and hetero-geneous amount of content, which we previously experienced through a very different medium. What will, for example, be the 'page ranking' of archived news? How will news, articles and chapters be internally ranked as first or last in response to a query? There are no incoming or outgoing links here, only Google's internal (and undisclosed) policies and methods, so once again it will be Google's decision, based on its own business convenience, strategy, and (one can only hope) vision.

As Google's own Nikesh Arora (President of Global Sales Operations and Business Development) stated quite plainly: the goal of Google's founders is "to create a universal library".[261] Marin Šarić (one of Google's top engineers and an initiator of the Google Books project, who eventually left the company after almost five years) revealed that Google considers 'worldwide culture' to include about 150 million books (the final scanning goal), and that by 2030 everything ever writ-ten will be online.[262]

But rather than the dream of some contemporary 'Library of Alexandria', this goal seems more like an unprecedented business op-portunity: selling advertisements to be displayed whenever someone reads a book selected from Google's vast online library, in the already-classic Google style: benevolent and fatherly. However, Google's ap-proach raises two serious concerns. First of all, access to this vast body of global culture is controlled and regulated by Google, a private mul-tinational business, instead of by a non-profit international institution such as UNESCO (which, incidentally, is running its own *World Digital Library* project, featuring a comparatively small number of digitised treasures[263]). Secondly, Google tends to focus on acquiring the most 'universal' (i.e. popular) types of culture, disregarding entire sectors of crucial, though less popular, printed productions. The acquisition and digitisation of this unprecedented amount of content, conducted with all the speed and efficiency of a huge corporation, is thus destined to become yet another 'gold mine' for selling context-sensitive web ads, and of course another endless temptation for our intellectual curiosity.

Let us consider the rival project: the Internet Archive's *Texts Collection* which in 2011 reached the figure of approximately three mil-lion books,[264] digitised in eighteen scanning centres in five countries. The project was originally funded with a grant of one million U.S. dollars by Microsoft. Eventually Microsoft pulled out of the project, leaving the Internet Archive all the scanning equipment and public-domain files. Soon enough, people started downloading public-domain books from Google Books and uploading them to the Internet Archive text collection.

A company called reCAPTCHA has developed another method for helping the Internet Archive effort, specifically its proofreading task: a variation of the widespread CAPTCHA system. CAPTCHA is a challenge/response system that allows Internet servers to distinguish a human user from a software 'bot' (an automated program, usually designed to generate spam) by asking the user to correctly type a displayed (and visually distorted) word. ReCAPTCHA uses a similar system, but adds a second word, one which was not conclusively recognised by the OCR (optical character recognition) software used to digitise books for the Internet Archive. When three human users have identified a word in the same way, the word is officially 'recognised' and inserted in the text.[265]

So the Internet Archive relies not only on public and private funding, but also on the support of individual or collective initiatives. Significantly, in May 2007 the U.S. State of California officially recognised the Internet Archive as a library, eligible for federal and state funding: for the first time, a library has been defined not as a physical building serving a geographically defined public, but as an abstracted digital space serving a huge worldwide community.[266]

But besides 'merely' digitising every book ever published, the Internet Archive also aims (in contrast with Google) to create a physical archive for the long-term preservation of the original printed books, the "authentic and original version that can be used as a reference in the future."[267] The plan and strategy, published in great detail online, is to keep one copy of every book and media acquired, until eventually the archive includes a physical and digital version of every work ever published. The books are to be catalogued and boxed, and stored in shipping containers modified to maintain controlled ideal environments of 10-15 degrees Celsius and 30% relative humidity.[268]

The Internet Archive has also set up another project called The Open Library, which aims to create an online database of every book ever published (featuring bibliographic details, summaries and tables of contents, all entered by users) – something of an open-source version of WorldCat, the worldwide database integrating the catalogues of more than ten thousand libraries, totalling 150 million records. The final piece of the Internet Archive puzzle is the Open Content Alliance, a collaborative effort of public institutions and corporations whose stated goal is to "build a permanent archive of multilingual digitized text and multimedia material".

The Internet Archive's founder Brewster Kahle describes his vision as follows:

> "Most societies place importance on preserving artifacts of their culture and heritage. Without such artifacts, civilization has no memory and no mechanism to learn from its successes and failures. Our culture now produces more and more artifacts in digital form. The Archive's mission is to help preserve those artifacts and create an Internet library for researchers, historians, and scholars."

On a smaller and more focused scale, various independent efforts appear to be following a similar approach. For example, the library of the University of Pennsylvania (sponsored by Kirtas Technologies, a scanning and digitisation business), is scanning its 200,000 public-domain titles, and selling copies through a print-on-demand service. The Emory University is also digitising and uploading public-domain titles (beginning with those selected by its librarians), so that scholars can access the texts online for free – or order a print-on-demand edition, the proceeds of which are used to cover the costs of the digitising programme.[269] Furthermore, there are several independent and peer-to-peer efforts designed to collectively share high-quality scans of books, such as the popular Gigapedia.com (recently renamed Library.nu) which hosts some 420,000 books in searchable and freely downloadable form.[270] And even the Holy Grail of theoretical and philosophical texts – the galaxy of academic papers and books produced since the 19th century – is being digitised in an apparently collective process and posted on the subversive website AAAAARG.ORG.[271] On the other end of the spectrum, we find digital archives being sold as a 'product', such as the *The Playboy Cover to Cover Hard Drive* which collects all 650 issues of *Playboy* magazine up until 2010: 56 years, 100,000 pages, on a single custom-designed hard disk, for $299.95.[272]

All these initiatives produce readable scanned images of book or

magazine pages, as well as searchable OCR-generated text, both of which can be accessed through formats such as PDF as well as online viewing. But the question remains: does any of this really qualify as 'archiving'? In purely technical terms it probably does. On the other hand, we must also take into account the intrinsically unsteady nature of digital data: there is still no long-term (or even medium-term) preservation technology for digital data that guarantees data integrity for even as little as 50 years in ideal conditions. And conditions are often far from ideal; data can easily become corrupted for any of a number of reasons. The media itself might be damaged (de-magnetised, de-layered, scratched, broken, etc) or exposed to environmental factors (sun, heat, electromagnetic interference, humidity, bacteria, smoke, etc); or the hardware or software required to read, decode, or decompress the data may no longer be available for whatever reason. Likewise, the data may become inaccessible (though not actually lost) if some essential network node is 'down', or if any of the network's various technologies is malfunctioning and no longer being maintained.

Meanwhile, the durable printed copies can still be found in libraries worldwide, where nothing short of some catastrophic physical accident can 'delete' them. The oldest surviving printed copy of a book (the *Diamond Sutra*) was block-printed more than 1,100 years ago, in 868 CE; the earliest known preserved writings, on clay tablets, are several thousand years old. One rare case of a new medium developed specifically for extremely long-term data storage is the *Rosetta Disk*:

> "Inspired by the historic Rosetta Stone, the Rosetta Disk is intended to be 'a durable archive of human languages' (...) Made of nickel alloy (with a 2,000 year life expectancy), the physical Disk is three inches across, and micro-etched with over 13,000 pages of language documentation, covering over 1,500 languages."[273]

On the other hand, the collective memory of contemporary society is extremely vulnerable, preserved on magnetic hard disks with ever-increasing storage densities (now over 200 gigabits per square inch). The only reasonably effective (short-term) strategy is to keep multiple backup copies in different physical locations – something only large corporations such as Google can afford to do on an industrial scale.[274] And although a digital copy can be deleted within a second, multiplying access to scanned documents by spreading copies (stored on different computers and at dif-

Rosetta Disk micro-etched with over 13,000 pages of language documentation, 2009

ferent locations) can possibly help to preserve them in our collective memory. Seen from the perspective of such (unfortunately very realistic) doomsday scenarios, the digitising of printed sources should not be considered as 'archiving' in any real sense, but merely as a method of 'accessing' the content ('access' is in itself a superlative buzzword, and of course the sheer thrill of being able to remotely access important printed content is certainly a major incentive for these huge ongoing 'archiving' efforts).

All good intentions aside though, we would do well to remember the vision expressed by the famous Argentine author and librarian Jorge Luis Borges, an undisputed literary master, in his timeless short story *The Library of Babel*.[275] This fictitious library is in fact a complete (and inhabited) universe: a seemingly endless grid of interlocking hexagonal rooms all filled with bookshelves. The narrator describes how "like all men of the Library, I have travelled in my youth; I have wandered in search of a book, perhaps the catalogue of catalogues." This library universe described by Borges illustrates the utopia of a finite index of the whole of human knowledge; as a compass, or a directory, of everything ever written and published. It also reminds us of the spiralling vastness of language in all its infinite variations. The utopia of a library of libraries is, in fact, disturbingly similar to the utopian vision propagated by the previously mentioned 'online giants'. Is it feasible (or even desirable) to definitively organise the whole of human knowledge (in its most traditional and extensive form: the printed word) in an ordered, searchable and indexable form? In Borges' short story, this vision turns out to be unmanageable, requiring an effort that stretches out into infinity: indeed, a library of Babel. Since it carries every single conceivable book (given a finite amount of letters, the number of books of finite length is not infinite), the library theoretically contains the solution to every imaginable problem – the only catch is that there's no way to find it, making the whole library in fact useless: "the certitude that some shelf in some hexagon held precious books and that these precious books were inaccessible, seemed almost intolerable."[276] Perhaps this a frustration that we in our 'age of information' can somehow identify with.

5.2   PRESERVING INDEPENDENT MAGAZINES, A CONTROVERSIAL STRUGGLE.

The desire to resurrect printed texts that have been lost or forgotten is as old as printing technology itself. As Marshall McLuhan once noted:

> "Indeed the first two centuries of printing from movable types were motivated much more by the desire to see ancient and medieval books than by the need to read and write new ones. Until 1700 much more than 50 per cent of all printed books were ancient or medieval."[277]

Paper has always been perceived as a stable extension of human memory, 'platform-independent' though physically limited. Following the major efforts by libraries to preserve books and magazines using microfilm technology (beginning in the mid-20th century), today's countless (personal) initiatives for preserving out-of-print or otherwise lost books and magazines make use of home scanners, OCR software and the PDF standard. The resurrection of forgotten or hard-to-find materials from the past stems from a widespread need to reconstruct, to reassemble, even to somehow re-enact the original publishing gesture; a need which obviously goes much deeper than the mere thrill of exploiting new technological possibilities. Nevertheless, the tools and methods used in this process of resurrection are in themselves significant.

One of the most celebrated underground press 'resurrections' was that of *Radical Software*. All eleven issues of this magazine (originally printed in the 1970s) were scanned, OCR-converted and reassembled in PDF format, and made available online for free; a significant resource for researchers and scholars of media culture worldwide. The whole process was funded by the Langlois Foundation – which focused its efforts on this one particular magazine, as it was considered to be probably the first media art magazine ever published. Several other magazines, particularly older ones, have been the subject of similar online 'resurrections'. For example, all issues of *L=A=N=G=U=A=G=E*, one of the most important magazines for experimental poetry, published in the U.S. in the 1970s, are now available online in the form of scanned images and PDF files (neither of which are searchable as text).[278]

A different approach was chosen for *Photostatic Retrograde*, a magazine published from 1983 to 1998 which focused on photocopying (xerography) as the source of a particular visual language. Every single issue, starting with the ones most recently published, was converted

Left
Cover of
Radical Software,
Volume I,
Number 5,
Spring 1972

Right
Cover of
*Photostatic
Retrograde*,
issue #1,
August 1983

to a (searchable) PDF file and made available online for free.[279] When the original lay-out (whether in the form of digital files or analogue materials) was no longer available, it was reconstructed from scratch. In this case, the act of archiving and preservation required a complete re-creation of the original printing plates (this time in a virtual, digital form) – resulting in a copy which was, paradoxically, 'better' than (or at least technically superior to) the original.

Traditional archiving can be defined as the preservation for historical memory of original materials, in a condition that is as historically accurate as possible. And so Jeff Rothenberg, digital data preservation expert for Rand Corporation, may well be right when he predicts that books in the future will no longer be considered as we know them today, but rather as 'art objects'.[280] Small publishers tend to regard the Web as a sort of global bookshop where they (often desperately) hope to attract customers. But these publishers' greatest asset is often their own history: their best and most successful books. Arguably their time and efforts would be better spent, not on producing unfocused blogs or unused internet forums, but on making their past treasures available and searchable online (or, at very least, a comprehensive reference to these old and out-of-print treasures: bibliographic references, cover images, tables of contents and summaries, etc). Besides increasing their own visibility (and thus attracting customers), such an archiving effort would also allow these publishers to support and preserve their own cultural context – the 'scene' which they previously played such an important role in describing and defining.

5.3 DISTRIBUTED ARCHIVES, THE PEER-TO-PEER ARCHIVE MODEL.

Often the only places where out-of-print or small-press books and magazines can still be found, are in private collections: little cornucopias of specialised knowledge, and clearly an important part of the history of their various cultural environments. Yet such collections are mostly unavailable online, simply because there is still no suitable platform to facilitate the necessary 'archiving' (or more accurately, 'accessing') process.

Within any literary, artistic or musical movement or 'subculture', there are usually a small number of readily identifiable individuals (journalists, historians, collectors, obsessive fans) or small institutions who have spent years assembling impressive collections, which subsequently just sit there collecting dust somewhere in a room (or a few rooms). Though the precious heritage is (individually) preserved, it remains invisible to the rest of the scene, and of course the rest of the world. But such content could also be shared, making it a publically available common resource, which in turn could significantly increase a publisher's online presence, not to mention its place in history. So besides preserving the material in the physical sense, collectors can also help increase its public presence, by sharing online as much of its content as technically and legally possible.

Using open-source and do-it-yourself (DIY) book scanning technology, developed in recent years by a small, scattered community of tinkering inventors and open-source programmers,[281] it is now relatively easy to quickly scan entire books, extract (OCR) their text, and make it available online (Google of course uses industrial technology for its Google Books programme). It is interesting to note that this community consistently applies an open-source methodology to the entire technical process – sharing not only the software, but also detailed hardware building instructions as well as the overall methodology. This represents a technological tipping point, since these machines, once built and distributed, will substantially speed up the process of digitising entire series of books or complete collections of independent magazines.

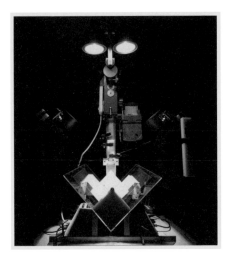

One of the many
different models of the
open-source project *DIY
Book Scanner*, 2010

The resulting repositories and databases, covering a wide variety of topics, could be made collectively searchable using simple (and free) software, which periodically surveys and indexes the content of each archive and makes it easily accessible through a dedicated search engine. The result: independent 'islands' of archived culture, gradually emerging and growing all across the Internet – all created by individuals sharing a passion, wishing to share information, and contributing to making accessible important content, currently unavailable on the Web. In other words, a collective memory, in much the same way as peer-to-peer networks have proven to be: combining the stability of our 'static' printed culture with the ephemeral (and thus dynamic) properties of digitisation.

Where institutions are characterised by a top-down approach (which usually makes their various databases incompatible, and thus difficult to integrate), the distributed archive follows a bottom-up model. Casting aside the museum and its monument-oriented outlook, a large number of culturally proactive individuals could all assume responsibility for their 'own' bit of culture, before eventually passing it on to another concerned party. Such an undertaking requires permanent 'seeders' (to return to the peer-to-peer parallel), individuals responsible for keeping the content available at all times. 'Seeding', in peer-to-peer terminology, means that in order to 'own' something, one has to share it (and whether the actual content itself is made available, or merely a reference to it, the mechanism remains much the same).

This of course is something entirely different from the whole 'nostalgia' industry. Building such archives of references, and digitising small and independent publications (while respecting the wishes of the original publishers and authors) would make it possible to reconnect fragments that were lost over time – and would allow precious texts, lent and never returned, to resurface. And so 'distributed archives', maintained through a peer-to-peer model, would constitute a community-based, free and shared model of preserving culture, as opposed to both the centralised bureaucratic public institution on one hand, and the equally centralised, quick and efficient commercial corporation on the other.

5.3.1. *The need for a 'flowable' archive form*

Wikipedia is now clearly the largest single global effort for sharing knowledge – but from a general, non-specialist, perspective, leaving plenty of gaps to be filled by countless specialised, independent (but networked) online archives of previously printed content. Meanwhile, access to such archives is increasingly becoming the norm among scholars, who need to efficiently and comprehensively search through huge quantities of information. Libraries increasingly prefer online magazine subscriptions to printed ones – simply because they're running out of space to store all the back issues. And the new online services that sell digital subscriptions to printed publications, often demand from publishers at least a minimum online back catalogue archive, in order to establish the publisher's online presence (as well as their own).

Online archiving has also had a major impact on the online presence of various newspapers – such as the *New York Times*, which famously archived every single one of its 13 million published articles, making them all available online for free (in plain text format), or for a fee (including photos, graphs, etc).[282] Here again, the keyword is access: the availability of a large amount of sources and data offers a broader perspective on any given phenomenon.

The online presence of small publishers is still largely inadequate, and does not at all present a clear picture of either their historical production, or the cultural context they are currently a part of. This is because such publishers have generally regarded the Web as merely a sales tool, rather than a platform which might enable them to expand the cultural presence they already enjoy in the real 'offline' world. What is needed here is a paradigm shift: independent publishers should consider the Web not merely in terms of sales, but also in terms of archive-building, exposure and sharing. In this context, personal and independent online archives must be considered as independent virtual 'servers', potentially interconnected and collectively searchable.

The presence of such archives could slightly tip the balance between net and paper in an online economy, with a positive effect on the visibility and availability of printed history.

So what exactly is the value of digital archiving, other than some expanded version (again, mainly in terms of access) of 'old-fashioned' microfilm archiving? In the case of digitally generated content, it means that a reproduction can actually be identical to its 'original'. Geoffrey Batchen wrote in his 2006 essay *The Art of Archiving*:

> "The archive is no longer a matter of discrete objects (files, books, art works, etc.) stored and retrieved in specific places (libraries, museums, etc.). Now the archive is also a continuous stream of data, without geography or container, continuously transmitted and therefore without temporal restriction (always available in the here and now)."[283]

After more than fifteen years of using the Web, we have grown accustomed to typing in search terms and almost instantly having the resulting texts delivered to our screen – to the point where such instant accessibility has become a prerequisite for considering any text as a quotable source, or as usable 'content'. But 'searchability', despite all its obvious benefits, is no replacement for our own photographic memory, and our innate human ability for making connections between various sources. A typical bibliography at the end of a book is in fact much more sophisticated than even the most ingenious 'advanced search', since it is the result of a thoughtful and time-consuming effort of searching and making connections – a process which is fundamentally different from the mere linking of items through search terms or similar queries by other users, which relies only on direct, explicit links. But our brain is of course much more subtle and sophisticated than that; the associations (or 'links') it is able to make are based on the abstraction of experience, sometimes even on sheer instinct. And such processes are notoriously difficult to codify in universal algorithms. As Marshall McLuhan stated in *Understanding Media*: "Plainly, to store is to expedite, since what is stored is also more accessible than what has to be gathered."[284]

5.4   THE ART OF THE ARCHIVE:
       HARD-COPYING THE DIGITAL DATABASE.

Conceptually, an archive can be considered as a substantial quantity of raw material (data) to which further transformations may be applied.

Art, and more specifically media art, often deals with archives and their intriguing content (data which is connected yet heterogeneous) – still, the attitude of artists, when referring to paper archives, seems to be to approach them from a retrospective point of view. An artist referring to an archive will usually depict its traditional, physical form, which is undoubtedly still the one we're most familiar with, even after a few decades of computers and databases.

For example, Cody Trepte's installation *1 Year of Archived Email*[285] consists of stacks of a few thousand punched cards (the oldest computer storage medium), on which an entire year of personal e-mail has been archived. The artist chose here a hybrid representation: the e-mail messages are indeed 'archived' (stored on punched cards, in much

the same way as if they had been recorded on a modern magnetic or optical computer storage medium such as floppy or hard disk, CD or DVD). But they are also in a certain sense 'printed', since they are visibly reproduced on paper (though the cards are not in any normal sense readable by humans; the digital encoding is designed to be deciphered by a machine). The artist in his statement tells us how computers "have become machines for remembering"; it is also interesting to note that punched cards are actually the most durable form of computer storage. The installation also contains some manually written (and almost equally cryptic) indexes: for example, the exact date and time each e-mail message was sent or received, which uniquely identifies each message, while the content of the messages themselves remains unreadable – in plain view, yet inaccessible. As with other conceptually similar artworks, we are shown here what happens when the sheer amount of data involved – which was made invisible inside the computer's hard disk – suddenly reveals its full spatial dimension.

A similar approach was chosen by Tim Schwartz for his installation *Card Catalog*:[286] a single drawer, more than 2 metres long, filled with index cards cataloguing all of the 7,390 songs on the artist's iPod, one card for each song. In this case the data is human-readable, though it is not a representation of the actual content (there are no scores or other musical data) but merely of its complete index. Here too, the author reflects on the notion of space (both real and virtual): the paper catalogue is incomparably larger than the actual musical content of the tiny MP3 player. Significantly, the installation was constructed as a classic wooden 19th century-style filing card cabinet with a brass knob, reminding us that the paper catalogues we have been using for centuries in old libraries can still serve to represent knowledge in a universally recognisable format – while on the other hand, the actual workings of something like a hard disk are still completely invisible and arcane to most of us. This aspect was further emphasised by ordering the cards chronologically, according to the history of the artist's listening selections, thus creating an even closer correspondence between the invisible data and its paper index.

This physical imbalance between digital content and its physical (printed) representation is also a theme of two other artworks: Rob Matthews' *Wikipedia*,[287] a 5,000-page book collecting articles featured on Wikipedia, and Mike Bouchet's *Almost Every City in the World*,[288] a 30,000-page "list of almost every city, town, village, or named liv-

Clockwise starting left

Rob Matthews,
Wikipedia, 2009

Mike Bouchet, *Almost Every City in the World*, 2005

A detail of the *Amazon Noir* installation, 2008

ing location in the world". In the first case, the question we are invited to reflect upon is mostly one of scale: the content which was invisibly registered on magnetic memory becomes excessively abundant once it is rendered physically. In the second case, we are confronted with the problem of completeness within a single standard format (the book). Both works in their own way deal with the notion of printing out a database as a means of somehow 'archiving' it.

Another artwork about books in their archived form is *Amazon Noir*, which I developed in collaboration with the Italian artist Paolo Cirio and the Austrian artist couple Ubermorgen. Our plan was to explore the boundaries of copyrighting text, and to examine the intrinsic technological paradox of protecting an electronic text from unauthorised copying. As mentioned earlier, Amazon features a powerful and attractive marketing tool called 'Search Inside the Book' which allows potential customers to search the entire text of a book; *Amazon Noir* merely exploited this mechanism by stretching it to its own logical conclusion. Paolo Cirio designed software to obtain the entire text and then automatically save it as a PDF file – once we had established the first sentence of the text, the software then used the last words of this sentence as a search term for retrieving the first words of the next sentence. By reiterating this process (a total of 2,000 to 3,000 queries for an average book) and automatically reconstructing the fragments, the software ended up collecting the entire text.

In order to better visualise the process, we created an installation: two overhead projectors displaying the project's logo and a diagram of the internal workings of our software, and a medical incubator containing one of the 'stolen' (and digitally reprinted) books. The book we chose to 'steal' was (of course) *Steal This Book*, the 1970s counterculture classic by the American activist Abbie Hoffman. In a sense, we literally 're-incarnated' the book in a new, mutated physical form. But we also put up a warning sign near the incubator:

> "The book inside the incubator is the physical embodiment of a complex Amazon.com hacking action. It has been obtained exploiting the Amazon 'Search Inside The Book' tool. Take care because it's an illegitimate and premature son born from the relationship between Amazon and Copyright. It's illegitimate because it's an unauthorized print of a copyright-protected book. And it's premature because the gestation of this relationship's outcome is far from being mature."

Our installation demonstrated a networked and digital process – but without actually displaying any digital technology. As for the book itself, it was effectively metamorphosed twice: the first time when Amazon disembodied (digitised) the book in order to make it available (in fragments) on its own servers; and the second time when we stole this digitised version and re-incarnated the book, in a form as close as possible to the original. In fact, Amazon has similarly disembodied a substantial amount of the books it sells, resulting in a very sizeable database indeed. And in a way, it is clearly understood that the entire content is in fact freely available, just a few mysterious mouse-clicks away. So Amazon is hosting a cornucopia of texts, an astonishing amount of knowledge, a compelling body of culture – all of it infinitely put on hold for marketing reasons.

We asked ourselves: what's the difference between digitally scanning the text of a book we already own, and obtaining it through *Amazon Noir*? In strictly conceptual terms, there is no difference at all, other then the amount of time we spent on the project. We wished to set up our own Amazon, definitively circumventing the confusion of endless purchase-inducing stimuli. So we stole the hidden and disjointed connections between the sentences of a text, to reveal them for our own amusement and edification; we stole the digital implementation of synaptic connections between memories (both human and electronic) created by a giant online retailer in order to amuse and seduce us into compulsive consumption; we were thieves of memory (in a McLuhanian sense), stealing for the right to remember, the right to independently and freely construct our own physical memory.

5.5   SCRAPBOOKS, GRASSROOTS ARCHIVING
       AS A NEW METHODOLOGY.

Scrapbooking is a method of preserving personal history by collecting printed clippings, photos, cherished memorabilia and other artefacts in blank books or notebooks. Though its exact origins are uncertain, scrapbooking is probably as old as print itself. The earliest references to the phenomenon are from 15th-century England, where 'commonplace books' were a popular way of compiling information such as recipes, letters, poems, etc. Then in the 19th century (particularly in the U.S.) a different kind of scrapbook made its appearance, owing to the novelty of newspapers and magazines which were suddenly very widespread and much cheaper than books. The timeless problem of stacks of paper taking up precious space could be deftly solved by clipping out what was worth keeping, and compiling personal selections of what today might be referred to as 'press reviews', to be saved and sometimes even re-circulated – "occasionally privately printed and circulated among friends", as Ellen Gruber Garvey noted in her essay *Scissoring and Scrapbooks*.[289]

Although the author Mark Twain marketed his patented pre-glued scrapbooks, most scrapbook practitioners would use old or otherwise uninteresting books (such as free annual reports) as the physical basis for their collections of clippings.[290] According to Garvey, scrapbooks stem from the "desire to mark the path of one's own reading". The limited space of the scrapbook allows only a finite (and thus necessarily rigorous) selection from many available sources, resulting in a new composition: a repository of personally relevant content.

A 19th-century
scrapbook

We could also consider this phenomenon as an early (and analogue) version of the current trend of 'personal authoring' made possible by the Internet and its stockpile of free authoring tools for web pages, blogs, social networks, etc. For most of the 20th century (with the notable exception of its last few years, when the digital era began) scrapbooks were used by fans to collect and preserve personal archives of clippings and photos of their favourite movie stars and pop idols: they were, in other words, repositories for the personal conservation of 'scraps' of memory. All of this was done in a state of blissful ignorance of the constraints of copyright – freely re-assembling clippings from a variety of sources and recombining them into new collections. (Incidentally, this phenomenon should not be confused with the somewhat related concept of diaries, which usually deal with strictly personal themes and sources rather than outside ones.)

To quote once again Ellen Gruber Garvey: "all media, old or new, are experienced as renewable resources".[291] And so, given a software tool that would enable us to cut out 'clippings' from electronic media and present them in a somehow 'traditional' way (clipping out exactly what we need without losing any of its technical or layout attributes), we would be able to filter the overwhelming quantities of information in an established manner and compile the result into (for example) PDF files. This would be fundamentally different from a collection of web bookmarks, which are in a sense much like physical bookmarks: they merely refer to the content, except (and this is a fundamental difference) that web bookmarks can be 'disconnected' and lost at any moment if the reference location happens to change or disappear. Digital scrapbooks, on the other hand, would enable users to compile entire books from clippings (by the way, there is software such as Evernote which allows the user to make 'web clippings', but only in a proprietary format which can't be shared, exported or incorporated in other publications).

And using print-on-demand technology, one could (again) produce real, physical scrapbooks, which would also be more or less instantly shareable. Such personal archives, the result of the individual sampling of content, could be connected to form a global archive of digital sources, collectively filtered by human passions and interests – a sort of cut-and-paste 'mashup' bootleg remixes. Imagine a scrapbook, filled with all the sources ('clippings') used in writing a book such as the one you're reading now, and presented independently of the medium in which they were originally published. Once the thorny issue of copyrights had somehow been settled (or circumvented, or blissfully ignored), such a scrapbook could then become the ideal starting point for anyone else wishing to continue and expand upon the original research.

CHAPTER 6

The network:
transforming culture,
transforming publishing.

A printed work of non-fiction, especially one which is part of a series (as are newspapers and magazines, as well as many books), is usually not meant to be an omni-comprehensive entity; it refers to external content, for example through quotes or bibliographical references. It can thus be seen as a 'node' within a broader network of cultural content; it may be a starting or ending point, though usually it will be one of many intermediary points on a longer path. Such connections have of course always existed; what the hypertext structure (on which most digital media is still based) adds to this, is not so much a new model, as rather an exponential increase in scope and speed. Furthermore, the network transforms the traditional paradigm of lone publishers (whether mainstream or independent), all locked in competition with one another as they create and distribute their products and try to get them sold. A fundamental re-conception of production and distribution schemes is necessary, in order to solve the dilemma of the publisher's relationship with the digital dimension. And this can best be done by adopting a characteristically digital strategy: that of the network.

6.1   THE MAGAZINE AS NETWORK NODE.

The most inspiring success stories of any 'underground culture' were never the accomplishments of any single prominent person or individual magazine, but of several of them together 'covering' a new scene and its flourishing culture. On a personal note, I have always considered *Neural* (the magazine which I have been editing since 1993) to be a single node within a larger network of productions, all delivering content on the same topic (in this case, digital culture). When I first started, I was fascinated by the emerging Internet, with its scattered yet interconnected structure; and I wondered just how this structure may become a model for other cultural efforts. In this early period, digital information and communication networks had just begun shifting towards the kind of real-time interaction which was already the norm in 'real-world' social structures: the active and reciprocal connection of various nodes collectively spreading information.

I soon realised that even in the 'horizontal' and egalitarian Internet culture of those early days, some nodes would always be 'more equal' than others; a collectively implemented process distinguishes important nodes from not-so-important ones, on the basis of their reputation. As Mathieu O'Neil pointed out in his book *Cyberchiefs*, the Internet may well be "a stateless system",[292] yet communities which have managed to produce outstanding results need to ensure

First issue of *Neural* magazine, November 1993

quality control, which can only be done by establishing some form of authority. In such contexts, the distribution of authority becomes synonymous with what O'Neil calls "the distribution of charisma"[293] – stripped (largely through the pioneering efforts of hacker groups) of the rigid hierarchies of more traditional meritocratic systems.

But developing charisma and building up reputation require time and effort, and in networked communication systems there is simply no excuse for poor quality; this gradually transforms the way a magazine is compiled and distributed. In the case of my own *Neural* magazine, the sheer challenge of putting together a new issue, with the best quality we can manage within the time and budget available, remains a powerful motivation for doing so in the first place. News of what is or isn't worth the time and effort (and in many cases, the money) of looking into spreads very fast online, and there are always plenty of alternatives when any given product no longer lives up to past expectations. In other words, the 'quality ecosystem' has been profoundly and permanently transformed by the rise of the Internet.

6.1.1   *Network means distributing, and distribution substantially benefits from the network.*

An important aspect of every publisher's mission is to spread its content. But setting up a distribution infrastructure, outside of the usual commercial channels, can be a major challenge. In England in the 1830s, the radical press in order to survive systematically evaded the exorbitant stamp bonds and duties (designed to limit publishing to "men of some respectability and property"[294]), relying instead on trusted 'underground' printers and running a well-organised independent distribution network, even establishing a collective fund for the families of those imprisoned for selling illegal 'unstamped' newspapers. The authorities responded by arresting unauthorised printers, intercepting paper supplies, and jailing retailers. From 1830 to 1836, a total of 1,130 cases of selling unstamped newspapers were prosecuted in London. In spite of this massive repression, the radical press flourished: total readership was estimated to be two million, well above that of the 'respectable' stamped press. Eventually the liberal Whig Party government reformed the policy, on one hand granting authorities even broader repressive powers, on the other hand reducing the stamp duty by 75% in order to make bootlegging less attractive, ultimately leading to increased freedom of press.[295]

Similarly well-organised infrastructures were set up by radical trade unionists in the West shortly before the Second World War, as well as by underground writers and political dissidents in the U.S.S.R. during the 1950s (see chapter 2.3). Such self-organised networks were able to grow and function without any access to sophisticated network technology; still, they functioned according to certain essential principles and structures characteristic of the network, including the element of reputation-based hierarchy. It is also interesting to note that Dadaist magazines were haphazardly distributed, whereas the Fluxus movement used its internal network as an efficient infrastructure for distribution.

The small and medium-sized underground media distributors which first emerged during the 1970s, gave rise in the 1980s and 1990s to a galaxy of mail-order initiatives capable of bringing their published content to a vast public, which lived mostly on the margins of mainstream society and could thus best be reached using the postal system (another functioning network). This concept in turn would prove fundamental to establishing the Mail Art movement, which was able to set up a global distribution system using nothing but active participants (network nodes) and the pre-existing postal system. Finally, heliographed fanzines such as the Italian publication *Insekten Sekte* were distributed using an unusual 'copyleft' model: after the initial print run, the original plates were passed on to other individuals who could print as many copies as they wished (and even sell them) without any obligation to the original publishers.[296]

In all of the above cases, the key concept of the network proved to be a crucial distribution practice, which made it possible to navigate (and survive) the perilous seas of the marketplace through the development of alternative strategies. And if the Internet has taught us anything at all, it's that there is no fixed limit to the combined power of many single (yet mutually supportive) nodes.

6.1.2 *The network as infrastructure:*
agencies, syndicating, and directories.

The Associated Press was founded in 1846, when a group of newspapers decided to invest jointly in a new medium (the telegraph) in order to speed up the collection and distribution of information.[297] The Underground Press Syndicate (see chapter 2.5) was conceived in a similar fashion, but adding to this the novel idea of free syndication of the content of some 60 magazines; this network model proved to be a success, because each node (magazine) contributed to spreading news otherwise censored or ignored by the mainstream media. In this case, every single node had the same rights and duties as any other; this absence of pre-constituted hierarchy in turn attracted more nodes, all of which were then better positioned to accomplish their mission of radical communication. A similar role was fulfilled by the Liberation News Service (see chapter 2.5). Being part of such a network gave each member access to the circulation and readership of every other member, thus multiplying the scale on which any given publication was able to distribute its information.

Another similar model of mutual support consists of collectively compiling lists of resources and distributing them within a specific community. The Punk scene spawned at least two excellent examples of such collections of resources, which inspired countless individuals and organisations. The first of these was arguably influenced by the earlier *Whole Earth Catalog* (featuring information on little-known yet essential resources necessary for living outside of mainstream society): in 1992, the Anarcho-Punk collective Profane Existence and the Punk zine *Maximumrocknroll* together published the first edition of *Book Your Own Fuckin' Life*, a directory of bands, distributors, venues and private houses where "touring bands or travelling punks could sleep and sometimes eat for free",[298] enabling an entire generation of Punk bands to travel, find their way in the world, and meet like-minded individuals.

In the same period, the 'riot grrrl' movement was emerging in the U.S. with popular bands such as Bikini Kill encouraging young women to form their own band, share skills and publish zines. The resulting wave of personal and often explicitly feminist zines was readily embraced by the ongoing Punk movement, with its tradition of political engagement. Within a few years the Grrrl Zine Network[299] managed to compile a resource-rich list of almost 1,000 zines and distributors from thirty countries, fostering contact between like-minded individuals and groups. In addition to this painstaking compiling of resources, the Grrrl Zine Network also facilitated zine workshops in community venues and non-profit organisations, aiming to empower teenage girls through the self-production of zines and artists' books. The network enabled a scattered scene of small, loosely organised publishing efforts to share their resources and methods, which especially for small players would make a crucial difference. Enjoying such mutual support helped all members develop their own unique qualities while remaining aware of the efforts of their peers.

6.1.3 The network as a means of political support and sustainable business: the Punti Rossi ('Red Points') project.

In the 1970s in Italy, a diverse and dynamic left-wing political scene brought about a period of intensive underground publishing activity (see chapter 2.6), as well as a new realisation among small publishers of politically-oriented material of the need to work together, in order to increase readership opportunities and to gain individual status through exposure to the wider audience of a network. Early efforts such as the *Lega degli editori democratici* ('League of Democratic Publishers') and the *Editoria Militante* ('Militant Publishing') groups quickly collapsed, all good intentions notwithstanding. The turbulent year 1977, when most of the country's universities were taken over by massive student sit-ins, saw a peak of publishing activity (including countless short-lived periodicals) as well as new collaborative efforts between independent publishers (see also chapter 2.6).

Bookshops, which often functioned as meeting points for a lively community, began to envision a different role for themselves, acting also as ad-hoc publishers or distributors; and from all these developments a new, fluid cooperative structure began to emerge. A few dozen bookshops, united in the *Punti Rossi* ('Red Points') organisation,[300] agreed to set up collective distribution and storage facilities, and to exchange (rather than buy and sell) publications amongst each other, thus avoiding the need to invest in costly opening inventories, while also ensuring a better, more focused and more widespread distribution. Each month, revenues after sales were centrally calculated, then locally distributed among publishers using the aforementioned collective facilities. This had the additional benefit of freeing publishers from the typical pressures by distributors (who demanded continuity of production, a minimum amount of titles, etc). Participating bookshops were able to carry a wide assortment of titles, increasing their reputation as valuable points of reference and fulfilling an important social function within their respective local communities. The organisation lasted for four years, holding well-attended annual national conventions.

6.2   COLLABORATION IS BETTER THAN COMPETITION: THE MAG.NET NETWORK.

Any network relies on the collective strength of its nodes; each single node, though potentially weak when isolated, is important (even vital) for the entire network – in other words, there's safety in numbers. And the entire network is much stronger than the sum of its single nodes. A network is also different from an association or a society; it implies that the exchange between nodes should be mutually beneficial.

Returning to my own experience with the magazine *Neural*, it has always been my conviction that no single magazine (especially an independent one) could exhaustively cover the subject of digital culture. A network of magazines, on the other hand, would allow for a richer and more interesting debate, while also helping to avoid the proletarian infighting sadly typical of so many subcultures. And so, when I was invited to attend an international meeting of independent publishers exploring digital culture through the printed medium, I enthusiastically accepted. In May 2002, in Seville (Spain), we founded, after a few days of discussions, the 'Mag.net - Electronic Cultural Publishers'

The three Mag.net readers ('experiences in electronic cultural publishing'), 2005, 2007, 2008

network.[301] Its founding members were Simon Worthington (*Mute*, London); Mercedes Bunz and Sascha Kösch (both *De:Bug*, Berlin); Fran Ilich (*Undo*, Mexico); Alessandro Ludovico (*Neural*, Bari, Italy); Georg Schöllhammer (*Springerin*, Vienna); Ieva Auzina (*RIXC* and

Acoustic Space, Riga); Slavo Krekovic (*3/4 Revue*, Bratislava); Kristian Lukic (KUDA Media Center, Novi Sad); Vladan Sir (*Umelec*, Prague); Joanne Richardson (*Subsol* and *Balkon*, Romania); Carme Ortiz and Mar Villaespesa (Think Publishing, Spain); Miren Eraso (*Zehar*, San Sebastian, and Think Publishing); Claudia Castelo (*Flirt*, Lisbon); Malcolm Dickson (*Streetlevel* and *Variant*, Glasgow, U.K.); Pedro Jimenez (*Cafeína*, Seville); Julian Ruesga (*Parabólica*, Seville).[302]

In our first year, after setting up a mailing list and initiating a number of internal discussions, we quickly learned an essential lesson, which allowed us to avert an early failure: not everything should be decided collectively. Members of a network can become over-critical of each other, while themselves failing to assume the responsibility of accomplishing the necessary tasks. And so we failed in several areas. We did not succeed in implementing a functioning 'collective subscription' (which in an experimental version had already attracted new customers) due to differences in publication frequencies and a general lack of coordination. We missed important funding application deadlines. We never even got started on the collective online shop, a planned software portal for displaying and selling all our products, including software for automatically administering sales revenues (while leaving it to each member to dispatch their respective orders).

But once we dropped the 'everything should be done collectively' approach, things started to work out. We established and maintained informal rules regarding the syndication of content, and the commissioning of content from each other. But perhaps our greatest success was in the sharing of knowledge: we met in person several times, and took turns giving workshops from which everyone learned, on topics such as Internet retail payment, print on demand, library subscriptions, etc. We were able to share our resources: sales outlets, distributors, printing and print-on-demand facilities, organisational practices and successful strategies (such as how to attract new subscribers).

Last but not least, a number of us, after meeting up for this specific purpose, were able to publish three readers on the relationship between offline and online publishing. There is still much to be done: for example, setting up a structure for collectively selling advertising space in all publications at once, which would allow us all to reap the benefits of our total readership figures (something which has already been done on the Web, for example by Culture Pundits and Federated Media). Hopefully someone will assume the task of doing this at some point in the future.

6.3 THE NETWORK AS A LARGE-SCALE EXPERIMENT: THE *DOCUMENTA 12 MAGAZINES* PROJECT.

Perhaps inspired by the Mag.net blueprint, one of its members, Georg Schöllhammer (curator and founder of *Springerin* magazine) in 2005 conceived (and was appointed curator of) the *Documenta 12 Magazines* project, which brought together independent art magazines from around the world during the 12th edition of the vast Documenta art exhibition and programme.[303] His original project was to set up a "collective worldwide editorial project", "publishing and discussing contributions – essays, interviews, photo reportage, features, interventions from artists and articles of fiction" creating "a network... that aims to explore and discuss topics of current interest and relevance (not only) to the Documenta 12 (three main topics): 'Is modernity our antiquity?', 'What is bare life?' and 'What is to be done?'"

Top
View of the *Documenta 12 Magazines* project exhibition, Kassel, Germany, 2007

Bottom
A screenshot of the collaborative open-source editing platform used for the *Documenta 12 Magazines* project, 2007

In the months preceding the Documenta event, three 'magazines' were to be published, featuring content selected and discussed by the editors through an online platform. This same platform would also be used to preserve all project-related content produced by all participating magazines, and to make this content accessible to the public; a sort of 'journal of journals'. And as if that weren't enough, the first draft of the project also envisioned how users would be allowed to compile their own 'magazines' by selecting content (possibly even available in several languages) and submitting it to a print-on-demand web interface.

The huge project started with a few 'regional editors' (closely coordinated by Schöllhammer and each assigned their own vast geographical area) organising trans-regional meetings in Hong Kong, New Delhi, São Paulo and Cairo. These meetings helped increase the visibility of independent art magazines in parts of the world where independent publishers cannot easily meet. Several of them wished to go further: to discuss subjects beyond the scope of Documenta topics, and to organise a meeting of all involved parties at some point during the Documenta event itself.

Then, apparently, Documenta curators Roger M. Buergel and Ruth Noack stepped in and assumed control of the project. The 'magazine' as originally envisioned was downgraded to three large-format books, featuring content selected by Buergel and Noack themselves, instead of by the magazine editors. Furthermore, the online content was no longer available to the public (though it remained accessible internally to the editors). The French magazine *Multitudes* decided to contribute in a different way, hijacking and twisting the three original questions into something arguably more relevant: "Is modernity (y) our aftermath," "Is bare life your apocalyptic political dimension," and "What is to be done after the D12 Bildung Programme?"[304]) *Multitudes* then set up a website featuring answers to these questions by several well-known artists. Schöllhammer himself stated that whatever the outcome, his vision had been "to create a field of open conflict and open controversy".[305] An event such as Documenta, with its week-long programmes of conferences and lectures, is of course also an excellent opportunity to meet colleagues who happen to live on the other side of the world (even though one ends up meeting only a few colleagues at any given event); and many new projects and ideas are the result of such encounters.

Perhaps the last word on the lack of visibility and participation of the many publications involved was by Patricia Canetti, editor of *Canal Contemporâneo* (Brazil). She created a Wikipedia entry on all participating magazines, with links to their respective websites, encouraging them to edit and add content in order to re-appropriate this promising but unrealised community.[306] In the end though, the full potential of this large-scale experiment (a collective, collaborative editing process involving possibly dozens of professional editors) was mostly squandered. In all fairness, it must also be noted that the tool (still accessible online) was never used in any way other than that requested by the Documenta organisation; another missed opportunity, in spite of the numerous chances to do so, as well as the obvious creative resources of the community of editors. Hopefully, since it was developed as an open-source tool, it will become publicly available sooner or later.

6.4 EXTERNAL SUPPORT NETWORKS, ASSISTING PUBLISHING GESTURES FROM FARAWAY.

Publishing cannot exist without distribution. And distribution means bringing content/objects to remote locations, where they can be noticed and hopefully enjoyed. But actually being able to deliver the content/objects to any desired location is still the most important difference between commercial and independent publishing. Various projects have developed different strategies for overcoming this obstacle. *Mute's More is More* is one of the most promising: "A web-based system for distributing independent media for sale at local outlets and events. Members can also input contact information about their local area; bookstores, meetings, gatherings, and share this with everybody to help build the distribution network further."[307] Even more importantly, *More is More* suggests the shipping of goods could be done using a "community courier service" accessing a collective database of relevant venues: empty space in the luggage of people going to events (such as festivals or conferences) can be used for shipping products free of cost, up to the weight limit set by the airline (usually 20 kg). Thus a voluntary distribution and support infrastructure, a 'parasitical' distribution of printed underground cultural objects, can be set up quite simply, by making good use of space systematically wasted during travelling.

External support was also essential for the success of Tim Devin's *i left this here for you to read* project.[308] Every month or so he produced a magazine, in no more than 50 copies, which was then distributed in 25 cities across the U.S. and Canada by a network of volunteers. The

Tim Devin, *i left this here for you to read*, 2008

copies were left in public spaces, on a park bench or a bus seat, free for whoever happened to find them. The magazine included short articles, images and objects small enough "to be stapled or taped to a page". Here the product seeks and finds the audience, instead of the other way round; and this unexpected encounter adds an emotional element which potentially fascinates the reader. Not so much an 'objet trouvé' as a message in a bottle, tossed into the waves of the endless means of urban communication, looking for its reader/owner and hoping to be fully enjoyed; a model of random communication and chance encountering of information, and strikingly similar to that which takes place every day all across the Internet.

The artist Sal Randolph pursued a similar strategy for his *Free Words Project*.[309] He printed 3,000 copies of his book *Free Words*, 2,500 of which have since been placed on the shelves of bookshops and libraries by a worldwide network of volunteers; the book is clearly labelled as 'free'. The text of *Free Words* is a list of 13,000 words; the copyright page declares that "No Rights are Reserved", meaning the text is in the public domain. In much the same spirit, but using the rather different medium of bookmarks (in the traditional, pre-Internet sense of the word), *NamelessleTTer*[310] is a "collaborative art bookmarking project, where bookmarks are made and stashed inside of library books, books in stores, etc."

Leaving unexpected goods in shops is a practice known as 'shop-dropping', and its unwritten etiquette dictates that the goods in question should clearly and explicitly be works of art. In this spirit, the London-based street artist Decapitator (who has gained a certain notoriety with his headless advertisement-parody artworks) 'dropped' copies of a modified *Rolling Stone* magazine (featuring a beheaded Shakira) inside the Barnes & Noble bookshop on New York City's Union Square.[311]

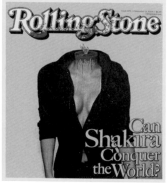

The original and the 'limited-edition decapitated' *Rolling Stone* magazine by Decapitator, 2009

The Canadian Institute for Infinitely Small Things applied an activist approach to the same strategy of infiltration with their *New American Dictionary: Security/Fear Edition*, leaving 40 copies of this book in libraries and bookshops in the city of Vancouver. The dictionary catalogues 67 American English terms related to fear and security which are either new or have taken on a new meaning in the post-9/11 era (Islamofascist, Freedom Fries, Friendly Fire, Regime Change, Smart Bomb, etc). The book was published through the print-on-demand service Lulu, making it automatically available for sale on Amazon.com.

Institute for Infinitely Small Things, *New American Dictionary: Security/Fear Edition*, 2007

All of these 'external support networks' showcase the possibilities of collectively infiltrating a distribution system. The effort of one single publisher is amplified, triggering a spectacular domino effect (each node of the network is able to find a way around another safeguard of the distribution infrastructure). In effect, such a network acts as a single complex organism. The network thus established is then able to perform a greater symbolic gesture, for which all nodes are equally responsible. It's a subversive form of distribution, but planned and focused in such a way as to multiply the effort of every single node.

6.5   THE NETWORK: THE FUTURE STARTS HERE.

If globalisation has meant the end of feudal markets, the network model (and particularly the Internet) has brought something more than merely new possibilities for passively receiving new broadcasted media, or feeding 'social network' platforms that capitalise on the aggregation of user's content; it has provided the infrastructure, as well as the inspiration, for setting up countless independent sub-networks, which make it possible for us to accomplish several independent tasks simultaneously.

Looking back at both ancient and recent history, we can see that the network is the most efficient and manageable structure for the support and distribution of publishing efforts. And so in publishing, we should consider not only networks of readers (whether they are discussing books on the extensive readme.cc online forum, or trading them without profit at BookMooch.com), but also networks of publishers and other active producers – promoting and distributing the result of their efforts using the opportunities only such a network can offer; involving readers, not merely as passive consumers, but as partners; and allowing digital products to freely circulate, creating a positive feedback loop (or 'virtuous circle') which in turn makes possible a new publishing experience.

In other words, the particular role of publishers within any cultural network (or even the entire network of human culture) is best fulfilled through free and open connection to other 'nodes' within that network. This is how we can generate meaning, and indeed bring some light, to the global network which we are now all a part of.

CONCLUSION

Post-digital print:
a future scenario

There is no one-way street from analogue to digital; rather, there are transitions between the two, in both directions. Digital is the paradigm for content and quantity of information; analogue is the paradigm for usability and interfacing. The recent history of video and music provides a good example, since the use of digital technology for these types of content is much more advanced than it is for publishing. In the case of video, the medium (whether VHS or DVD) is merely a carrier, since the content is always ultimately displayed on screens. The same is true for music, where cassettes, vinyl records and CDs are only intermediate carriers; the actual listening always happened through speakers (and increasingly through headphones). In both cases, the format changed without dramatically affecting the watching or listening experience. Sometimes the experience was improved by changes in the media technology (with HD video); sometimes it was almost imperceptibly worsened (with the loss of frequencies in MP3s).

Print, however, is a very different case, since the medium – the printed page – is more than just a carrier for things to be shown on some display; it is also the display itself. Changing it consequently changes people's experience, with all the (physical) habits, rituals and cultural conventions involved. E-publishing therefore still has a long way to go before it reaches the level of sophistication which printed pages have achieved over the course of a few centuries.

But as more and more content moves from print to digital, we seem to be approaching an inevitable turning point, where publishers soon will be releasing more electronic publications than printed materials. A key factor in this development is that e-publishing is gradually becoming just as simple and accessible as traditional publishing – not only for producers, but also, thanks to new interfaces, habits and conventions, for consumers as well. However, the real power of digital publishing lies not so much in its integration of multiple media, but in its superior networking capabilities. Even if it were possible to write some spectacular software to automatically transform e-books into another media standard (for instance, an animation of book or magazine pages being turned) or vice-versa, this would be far less interesting for users than new and sophisticated forms of connectivity – not only to related content hosted elsewhere, but also to other humans willing to share their knowledge online. To this end, digital publishing will have to establish universal interoperability standards and product identities that don't lock customers into the closed worlds of one particular application or service.

Traditional print publishing, on the other hand, is increasingly presenting its products as valuable objects and collector's items, by exploiting the physical and tactile qualities of paper. It thus acts as a counterpart to the digital world, while looking for ways to cope with a gradually shrinking customer base – particularly in its traditional sectors such as newspaper production and distribution (where costs are becoming unsustainable) or paper encyclopaedias (which have already become vintage status symbols rather than practical information tools). A number of products will thus need to be re-invented in order to still make sense in print.

At the time of writing, the development towards print as a valuable object can best be observed in the contemporary do-it-yourself book and zine scene. Until the late 1990s, this scene was mostly focused on radical politics and social engagement; the contemporary scene however is more fascinated with the collection of visual-symbolic information into carefully crafted paper objects. Despite its loyalty to print, this new generation of DIY publishers has created offline networks for print production and distribution which, in their bottom-up structure and peer-to-peer ethic, very much resemble Internet communities. At the same time, the work they create is meant to remain offline and not be digitised, thus requiring a physical exchange between publisher, distributor and reader. This ethic is squarely opposed to the so-called 'go all digital' philosophy[312] which advocates a completely digital life, getting rid of as much physical belongings as possible, and relying only on a laptop and a mobile phone filled with digitised materials.

For sure, the DIY print publishing ethic is closely related to the (often dormant) bottom-up social dynamics of the Internet. But as it currently stands, it still lacks one crucial aspect (besides production and sharing): it does not include mechanisms able to initiate social or media processes which could potentially bring the printed content to another level – what I would call the 'processual' level. In the past, print activism (using pamphlets, avant-garde magazines, Punk zines, etc) was deployed for spreading new ideas meant to induce new creative, technological and – by implication – social and political processes. The future of post-digital print may also involve new processes, such as remote printing, networked real-time distribution, and on-demand customisation of printed materials – all processes with (as of yet) unexplored social and political potential.

Conversely, digital networking technologies could make better use of print. Those who advocate and develop these new technologies should perhaps become more aware of print's cultural significance. Many readers will continue to choose print products above electronic publications, possibly leading to a demand for networked (perhaps even portable) printers allowing individuals to print materials at any location, anywhere in the world. Combined with personal binding devices (however primitive), such personal 'book machines' would allow readers to 'teleport' print publications to and from any location. Furthermore, resistance to the ubiquitous and non-stop surveillance of the Internet may well take a more radical turn: individuals and groups could make a political statement out of going completely offline and working in isolation as neo-analogue media practitioners.

If print increasingly becomes a valuable or collectable object, and digital publishing indeed continues to grow as expected, the two will nevertheless cross paths frequently, potentially generating new hybrid forms. Currently, the main constraint on the development of such hybrids is the publishing industry's focus on entertainment. What we see, as a result, are up-to-date printable PDF files on one hand, and on the other hand online news aggregators (such as Flipboard[313] and Pulse[314]) which gather various sources within one application with a slick unified interface and layout. But these are merely the products of 'industrial' customisation – the consumer product 'choice' of combining existing features and extras, where the actual customising is almost irrelevant. Currently, the industry's main post-digital print entertainment effort is the QR code – those black-and-white pixellated square images which, when read with the proper mobile phone app, give the reader access to some sort of content (almost always a video or web page). This kind of technology could be used much more creatively, as a means of enriching the process of content generation. For example, printed books and magazines could include such codes as a means of providing new updates each time they are scanned – and these updates could in turn be made printable or otherwise preservable. Digital publications might then send customised updates to personal printers, using information from different sources closely related to the publication's content. This could potentially open up new cultural pathways and create unexpected juxtapositions.

Martin Fuchs and Peter Bichsel's book *Written Images* is an example of the first 'baby steps' of such a hybrid post-digital print publishing strategy. Though it's still a traditional book, each copy is individually computer-generated, thus disrupting the fixed 'serial' nature of print. Furthermore, the project was financed through a networked model (using Kickstarter, a very successful 'crowdfunding' platform), speculating on the enthusiasm of its future customers (and in this case, collectors). In other words, this book is a comprehensive example of post-digital print, through a combination of several elements: print as a limited-edition object; networked crowdfunding; computer-processed information; hybridisation of print and digital – all in one single medium, a traditional book. On the other hand, this hybrid is still limited in several respects: its process is complete as soon as it has been acquired by the reader; there is no further community process or networked activity involved; once purchased, it will remain forever a traditional book on a shelf. And so, there is still plenty of room for exploration in developing future hybrid publishing projects.

When we are no longer able to categorise publications as either a 'print publication' or an 'e-publication' (or a print publication with some electronic enhancement), then the first true hybrids will have arrived. It may be worth envisioning a kind of 'print sampling', comparable to sampling in music and video, where customised content (either anthologies or new works) can be created from past works. Such a 'remix' publishing strategy could create new cultural opportunities, and open up new 'processual' publishing practices. We can already see this happening to some extent, in contemporary zine and DIY art book publishing, as well as underground e-book websites.

Since software is a prerequisite for any digital technology (and is also being used for the creation of most analogue works today), its 'processual' nature should be reflected in the structure and dynamics of future publishing: enabling local and remote participation, and also connecting publishing to real-life actions. The younger 'digital native' generation has no compunction in irreverently sampling, remixing and 'mashing up' traditional and social media (as several adventurous small organisations, born out of the current financial crisis and the 'Occupy' movement, have already demonstrated). Print is, unsurprisingly, an important component of this 'mashup', because of its acknowledged historical importance as well as its particular material characteristics. And so this new generation of publishers, able to make use of various new and old media without the burden of ideological affiliation to any particular one of them, will surely be in a position to develop new and truly hybrid publications, by creatively combining the best standards and interfaces of both digital and print.

Appendix

Print
vs.
electrons

100 differences and similarities
between paper and pixel.

PRODUCTION

1	Screen colour consistency	Cross-browser consistency
2	300 dpi	72 dpi
3	A(x), (e.g. A4)	(x)GA (e.g. XVGA)
4	Snap to grid	CSS constraints
5	Postscript I/O error	Error 404
6	Ethernet	Wi-Fi
7	Glowing ink	Flash (Adobe)
8	Image not found	Can't connect to server
9	Magnifying glass	Magnifying icon
10	Moiré	Excessive JPEG compression
11	nth colour	Custom programming
12	Pantone	Optimised palette
13	Stock photography	Google images
14	Proofreading	Debugging
15	Test print	Draft version
16	Higher resolution	Anti-aliasing
17	Page layout software	Content management system
18	Spines	Partial browser incompatibility
19	Optimising for print	Optimising for search
20	Cutting	Screen format
21	Recycled paper	White text on black screen
22	Hollow punch	Layers
23	PDF logo	JPEG logo
24	Advertising space	Banner
25	Paid promotional flyer	Pop-up window
26	Ink	Brilliance
27	Full-colour insert	Picture gallery
28	Imposition	Sorting with tags
29	Binding	Website structure

STRUCTURE (INTERNAL)

30	Colour addition	Colour subtraction
31	Centerfold	Background image
32	Contrast	Brightness
33	Dot	Pixel
34	TIFF	JPEG
35	PDF (fixed layout)	EPUB (reflowability)
36	vector graphics	Bitmap
37	front cover	Home page
38	externally illuminated	Backlit
39	local link	Remote link
40	paper weight	Download time
41	Plastification	Use of 3D/shadows
42	RAM	kbps
43	Best viewed in bright light	Best viewed in dim light
44	Fire damage	File corruption
45	Fibres	Waves
46	Turns yellow	Reveals its pixel matrix
47	Consumed in local time	Consumed in global time
48	Slow replication	Instant replication
49	Hardcover	Paid access
50	Paperback	Free access
51	Static	Cinematic

STRUCTURE (EXTERNAL)

52	Printer	Sysadmin
53	Barcode	WHOIS
54	ISSN	Online ISSN
55	Local storage backup	Remote server backup
56	Back catalogue	Internal search engines/archive.org
57	Optimised distribution	Optimised server configuration
58	Stocks	Link on the home page
59	Second (nth) edition	Database rebuilt
60	Headquarters	Hosting
61	Shipping strike	No connection

EVALUATION

62	Readership	Unique visits
63	Certified distribution	Guaranteed bandwidth
64	Distributor list	Access logs
65	Referenced by other media	Incoming links
66	Low copy/user ratio	High copy/user ratio
67	Promotional copies	RSS

REAL AND VIRTUAL SPACE

| 68 | Bookshelf | Database |
| 69 | Shelf space | Web host storage space |

CONVENTIONS

70	Table of contents	Menu
71	Promotional T-shirt	Textual link
72	Handwritten font	Pixel font
73	Captions	Alt text tag
74	News department	Blog
75	Page format	Scrolling
76	Print	Save
77	Bibliography	Hyperlinks
78	Name	Domain name
79	Paper bookmark	Browser bookmark
80	Page numbering	Posting date
81	Clippings	Cache
82	Import dialogue window	Online form

CONSUMPTION

83	Reader	User
84	Subscriber	Registered user
85	Subscription	Push technology
86	Reproduction prohibited	Digital rights management
87	Syndication	Creative commons
88	Freebie	Free download
89	Shipping	Spamming
90	Cover price	Password-protected access
91	Dust	Dust

GESTURES

92	Flipping through	Clicking
93	Smell of ink	Sound of mouse clicks
94	Photocopying	Copy/paste
95	Annotating	Comments
96	Underlining	Underlining
97	Fingerprint on coating	Fingerprint on screen
98	Folding	Scaling
99	Locally read	Remotely read
100	Handing over	Forwarding

Afterword

BY FLORIAN CRAMER

The American composer Kim Cascone, writing in the winter 2000 issue of *Computer Music Journal*, coined the term 'post-digital' to describe a certain type of electronic music which made playful use of technical digital glitches and was cheaply produced on laptop computers.[1] But what does 'post-digital' really mean in an age of digitisation – and as a description of a music which had in fact been digitally produced? Though Cascone's article confused media with tools, and promoted a false conflation of 'digital' with 'high tech', his main argument for a 'post-digital' media age still holds: "Because the revolutionary period of the digital information age has surely passed. The tendrils of digital technology have in some way touched everyone".[11] In a post-digital age, the question of whether or not something is digital is no longer really important – just as the ubiquity of print, soon after Gutenberg, rendered obsolete all debates (besides historical ones) about the 'print revolution'.

However, for many (if not most) people, the 'digital information age' did not become a fact of their everyday life until it moved from office computers to their smartphones. As an electronic musician, Cascone was about a decade ahead of his time. Music – with its historical (even ancient) ties to mathematics and computation, and its pioneering use of electronic media (from radio to MP3) – has always been the first art form to adapt to new information technologies. For the world of book and magazine publishing, however, the old-school 'revolutionary period' of the 'digital information age' is not yet over – in fact, it has only just begun. And so were are stuck, at the time of writing, in fruitless debates about the Web, e-readers and tablet computers – and the perceived or real threat of these technologies to the field of book, magazine and newspaper publishing.

One reason why this debate is so difficult to penetrate, is that it has become heavily ideological. In one camp, we have the usual web, network-culture and new-media evangelists; on the other side, people (usually from a fine-art or graphic-design background) who feel passionately about the tangible, material qualities of print. In reality, we are seeing a boom in zines, artists' books and artists' bookshops, quite comparable to the contemporary boom in Internet communities. And it would be wrong to dismiss this development as merely another

162

'retro' trend.[III] The zine and artists' book communities themselves are networked via blogs and Internet forums. Perhaps more significantly, they use print as a form of social networking which is not controlled by Google, Twitter or Facebook. These communities are thus an avant-garde of a new post-digital print culture – a culture in which the false dichotomy of 'print' versus 'electronic' (which has haunted us since McLuhan) is suspended.

This false opposition has been further amplified through the common conflations of 'print', 'book' and 'writing'. In his 1975 manifesto *The New Art of Making Books*, the Mexican-Dutch intermedia artist Ulises Carrión clarified that a "writer, contrary to the popular opinion, does not write books. A writer writes texts".[IV] Against a narrowly literary notion of the book, he comprehensively defined it as "a space-time sequence" that may "contain any (written) language, not only literary language, or even any other system of signs".[V] Carrión of course was making his case for the post-Fluxus medium of non-literary artists' books – or, to use his own, and much better, term, 'bookworks' – which he sold in his bookshop 'Other Books & So' on Amsterdam's Herengracht. His notion of books was abstract rather than material – a definition consistent with the early 20th century philosopher Ernst Cassirer's concept of the 'symbolic form'. And it is precisely such a symbolic form which is able to migrate, more or less painlessly, to an electronic medium (such as the e-book) – just as the 'symbolic form' of the music track or album has migrated back and forth between vinyl, cassette, CD, MP3, and Internet streaming.

Print, however, is not a symbolic form, but a medium in the most literal sense of the word; a physical carrier of information. Today's artists' books differ from those of Carrión's time in their shift from the linguistic to the tangible, from the symbolic form to the core medium,[VI] or from bookworks to printworks. This is the definition of print which we have been using for the purposes of the present book.

Besides being a rich account of the history of experimental publishing in parallel to that of modern art, this book also is a (covert) piece of personal storytelling. For more than twenty years, Alessandro Ludovico has been working at the cutting edge (and the outer fringes) of both print publishing and Internet community activism. Neural, the magazine which he edits, publishes and distributes, began as an Italian-language popular cultural glossy magazine focusing on cyber-punk culture, but gradually morphed into the major international news and information source on critical, counter-cultural and activist new-media arts which it is today. *Neural* has participated in collaborative efforts such as the *Documenta 12 Magazines* project (see chapter 6.3).

Still – and despite its subject matter and reader demographic – *Neural* magazine has never become an electronic publication, which is something of a statement in itself.

Since the early 20th century, Italy has been a real-life test laboratory for social and political developments which sooner or later hit the rest of the Western world. During Neural magazine's first two decades, Prime Minister Silvio Berlusconi personally embodied an unprecedented monopoly complex of mass media, publishing and politics, resulting in a sharp dichotomy between corporate and independent media. For Italy's artists, there is a similar gap between the contemporary-art-friendly but extremely commercial North of the country, and the conservative South where the official art system is all about cultural heritage. There, contemporary arts – including media experimentalism – have always been counter-cultural more or less by definition and, without any supporting institutions, have resorted to exhibiting and performing in squatted 'social centres'. In such a cultural climate, print and the Internet could be equally embraced as independent do-it-yourself media. They did not stand (as was the case in Northern Europe and North America) for two separate cultures and art communities.

In this book, Alessandro Ludovico re-reads the history of the avant-garde arts as a prehistory of cutting through these dichotomies. He shows how contemporary forms of networked publishing – using whichever medium or technology – were in fact prefigured by 20th and 21st century artists and their media experiments. Thus, his conclusion that 'print is liberating' is not a question of pitching one medium against another. His concept of media as a liberating force is also strongly informed by computer-hacker culture. In 2008, a collaboration with a group of artists (including the young hacker-artist Paolo Cirio and the Austrian artist couple Ubermorgen) resulted in the project *Amazon Noir – The Big Book Crime* (see chapter 5.4), a small software application that took advantage of Amazon.com's 'Search Inside the Book' feature in order to extract complete copyrighted books from the website. *Amazon Noir* is about communality, very much in the same way as print and paper are. In one case, file sharing; in the other case, the physical social sharing of paper between people in one room. But either of these notions of sharing would be reductive when considered separately from the other: file sharing would then boil down to cybernetic feedback loops; paper sharing would mean no more than a romanticism of local physical exchange. Separately, each of these two paradigms sums up the limitations and frustrations one can experience when spending time either at a hacktivist event or in an artists' bookshop.

In his 1980 article *Bookworks Revisited*, Ulises Carrión described two extremes in contemporary artists' books, which anticipated similar extremes for file sharing and printmaking: the de-materialised book aesthetics of conceptual art versus the material overkill of sculptural book objects such as Dieter Rot's *Literaturwurst* ('Literature Sausage'), a mass of torn-out magazine pages stuffed into a transparent plastic foil casing. Neither of them qualified, from Carrión's critical perspective, as a 'bookwork'. Rot dissolved the symbolic form of the book and made it extrinsic to the object, turning it into something which no longer lent itself to reading – and which did not qualify as an object "in which the book form is intrinsic to the work", the definition of bookworks which Carrión had taken over (and twisted) from the curator and MOMA librarian Clive Phillpot.[VII] Conceptual art books, on the other hand, lacked artistic engagement with the book form itself: "A comic book", writes Carrión, "or a newspaper, creates richer and more varied and changing conditions for reading than Art & Language publications". He thus considered them "plain book[s]" just like conventional novels and non-fiction.[VIII]

If we projected Carrión's notion of the bookwork upon the concept of post-digital print, then neither purely visual-tactile printmaking, nor a mere website or text file would 'qualify'. In positive terms, post-digital print would need to include networked community sharing which is both local/tangible and global/digital; the union of the two opposites of formation and in-formation. Alessandro's 2006-2008 project Mag.net, a network of 'electronic cultural publishers', sought to combine these two modes of sharing through hybrid electronic and print-on-demand publishing.

The present book is another such hybrid. It will be published partly as a traditional offset print book, partly through print on demand, and partly as an e-book distributed through various underground and overground publishing channels – including pirate electronic libraries such as AAAAARG.ORG, and artist-run bookshops.

This book was developed and written as part of a practice-oriented research project at the Hogeschool Rotterdam called 'Communication in a Digital Age', featuring conferences and research papers, bringing together (graduate) students with professionals in the arts, design and media, and organising various events and activities within as well as outside the school. All of which is deeply connected to the narrative of this book – we at the Hogeschool are, in other words, also working to develop non-traditional, hybrid practices of research and education, similar to those which Alessandro develops in the publishing world.

The book's references feature extensive web links, some of which I fear may already have expired by the time you are reading these words. I believe this shouldn't be seen as a deficiency, but rather as an invitation to use this book as a resource, and to complement it with your own findings.

And so, an experimental hypothesis for this publication might be: if print is indeed liberating, then start by sharing this book.

[I] Kim Cascone, 'The Aesthetics of Failure: "Post-Digital" Tendencies in Contemporary Computer Music', in *Computer Music Journal*, 24:4, 2000, pp. 12-18

[II] ibid.

[III] An exemplary critique of contemporary retro culture focusing on pop music: Simon Reynolds, *Retromania. Pop Culture's Addiction to Its Own Past*, Faber & Faber, 2011

[IV] Facsimile reprint in: Guy Schraenen (ed.), Ulises Carrión, *We have won! Haven't we?*, Museum Fodor & Museum Weserburg, 1992, p. 53

[V] ibid.

[VI] and thus from metaphysics to ontology.

[VII] Ulises Carrión, 'Bookworks Revisited', reprinted in: James Langdon (ed.), *Book*, Eastside Projects, 2010, no pagination

[VIII] ibid.

(Endnotes)

All web links accessed on March 30, 2012

1   http://www.businessinsider.com/chart-of-the-day-workers-employed-in-news-paper-publishing-2009-12
2   Standage, T. (1998) *The Victorian Internet*, Phoenix
3   http://en.wikipedia.org/wiki/Innocenzo_Manzetti
4   Uzanne, O. and Robida, A. (1895) 'La fin des livres' in *Contes pour les bibliophiles*, Ancienne Maison Quantin; http://www.gutenberg.org/ebooks/2820
5   'Villemard 1910 - En L'An 2000'; http://www.flickr.com/photos/amphalon/3368395546/in/set-72157615623434624/
6   http://www.nytimes.com/2010/04/11/books/review/Schuessler-t.html?pagewanted=all
7   Saper, C. (2009) *Bob Brown's The Readies*, Rice University Press
8   http://www.bbc.co.uk/archive/hg_wells/
9   http://www.bbc.co.uk/archive/hg_wells/12407.shtml
10 http://www.bbc.co.uk/archive/hg_wells/12409.shtml
11 McLuhan, M. (1964) *Understanding Media*, McGraw-Hill, p. 400
12 ibid.
13 17 Days: *The Story of Newspaper History in the Making* (1945), Prelinger Archives; http://www.archive.org/details/17DaysTh1945
14 ibid.
15 ibid.
16 McLuhan, *Understanding Media*, p. 89
17 ibid., p. 179
18 McLuhan, M. (1955) 'New Media As Political Forms' in *Explorations 3*
19 http://projects.chass.utoronto.ca/mcluhan-studies/v1_iss1/1_1art5.htm
20 McLuhan, *Understanding Media*, p. 237
21 ibid.
22 Sellen, A.J. and Harper, R.H.R. (2002) *The Myth of the Paperless Office*, The MIT Press
23 Norman, D.A. (1998) *The Invisible Computer*, The MIT Press
24 Licklider, J.C.R. (1965) *Libraries of the future*, The MIT Press
25 http://www.businessweek.com/technology/content/may2008/tc20080526_547942.htm
26 Coover, R. (1992) 'The End of Books' in *The New York Times Book Review*, June 21 1992, pp. 23-25
27 Borges, J. L. (1977) *The Book of Sand*, Plume
28 Landow, G.P. (1994) *Hyper/Text/Theory*, The Johns Hopkins University Press
29 http://www.desvirtual.com/thebook/english/
30 http://www.paperkiller.com
31 Coover, op. cit.
32 Hayles, N.K. (2002) *Writing Machines*, The MIT Press
33 http://en.wikipedia.org/wiki/Help:Books
34 http://www.guardian.co.uk/books/2012/mar/13/encyclopedia-britannica-halts-print-publication
35 Branwyn, G. (1997) *Jamming The Media*, Chronicle Books

36 http://en.wikipedia.org/wiki/Biblia_pauperum
37 http://historymedren.about.com/library/text/bltxtgermany10.htm
38 Schwartz, S. (1996) 'History of Zines' in Vale, V., *Zines! Volume I*, V Search
39 http://cronologia.leonardo.it/storia/biografie/marinet2.htm
40 Müller-Brockmann, J. (1971) *A History of Visual Communication*, Hastings House Publishers
41 http://it.wikipedia.org/wiki/L%27Italia_futurista
42 Echaurren, P. (1997) *Volantini Italiani*, AAA
43 Lissitzky, E. (1990) El Lissitzky, 1890-1941: *Architect, Painter, Photographer, Typographer*, Municipal Van Abbemuseum
44 Schwartz, op. cit.
45 Schwartz, op. cit.
46 http://en.wikipedia.org/wiki/Polish_underground_press
47 Hendricks, J. (1988) *Fluxus Codex*, Abrams Inc
48 ibid.
49 ibid.
50 Kataoka, M. (2007) *All About Laughter*, Mori Art Museum
51 Welch, C. (1995) *Eternal Network: A Mail Art Anthology*, University of Calgary Press
52 http://www.ubu.com/aspen/
53 Cohen, A. (1991) *The San Francisco Oracle (Facsimile Edition)*, Regent Press
54 Pivano, F. (1972) *Beat Hippie Yippie*, Arcana
55 Hollstein, W. (1971) *Underground*, Sansoni
56 Brand, S. (1969) *Whole Earth Catalog: Fall 1969*, Portola Institute
57 Held, J. Jr. (1998) 'From Dada to DIY: The history of Alternative Art Culture in the 20th Century' in *Factsheet Five #63*
58 Baroni, V. (1997) *Arte Postale: Guida al network della corrispondenza creativa*, AAA Edizioni
59 Becker, C. (1998) 'The Art of Zines' in *Factsheet Five #63*
60 http://en.wikipedia.org/wiki/Gocco
61 http://www.richardkostelanetz.com/invent/assembling.php
62 Alferj, P. and Mazzone, G. (1979) *I Fiori di Gutenberg*, Arcana
63 Marx, K., in *Neue Rheinische Zeitung No. 221*, February 1849
64 http://www.tommasotozzi.it/index.php?title=Bambina_Precoce_%281984%29
65 http://en.wikipedia.org/wiki/Between_C_&_D
66 Branwyn, op. cit.
67 Gunderloy, M. (1992) *The World of Zines*, Penguin
68 Markoff, J. (1995) 'If Medium Is the Message, the Message Is the Web' in *New York Times*, November 20, 1995, p. A1
69 Schwartz, op. cit.
70 http://newstweek.com/
71 http://nytimes-se.com/
72 Berardi, F. (1977) *A/Traverso*
73 Ćosić, V. (2001) *Net.art per se*, MGLC
74 Bolter, J. D. (2001) *Writing Space: Computers, Hypertext, and the Remediation of Print*, Lawrence Erlbaum Associates
75 Royal Commission on National Development in the Arts, Letters and Sciences, 1949-1951, Chapter V, Section 7
76 http://www.youtube.com/watch?v=5WCTn4FljUQ&feature=player_embedded
77 http://www.observer.com/2007/02/emtimesem-sulzberger-newspaper-will-be-around-for-a-long-time/

78   http://www.seattlepi.com/business/article/Seattle-P-I-to-publish-last-
     edition-Tuesday-1302597.php
79   http://www.businessweek.com/bwdaily/dnflash/content/oct2008/
     db20081028_224442.htm
80   http://www.channel3000.com/news/15244670/detail.html
81   http://www.mlive.com/news/ann-arbor/index.ssf/2009/03/
     ann_arbor_news_to_close_in_jul.html
82   http://www.msnbc.msn.com/id/29412240/ns/business-us_business/t/
     rocky-mountain-news-publishes-final-edition/
83   http://tucsoncitizen.com/morgue/2009/02/20/110550-citizen-likely-to-
     close-march-21-no-buyer-stepping-up/
84   http://www.psfk.com/2009/10/evening-standard-goes-free.html
85   http://www.mondaynote.com/2010/03/14/euthanazing-the-paper-not-yet/
86   http://jimmywales.com/2009/10/21/is-the-magazine-dead/
87   Meyer, P. (2004) *The Vanishing Newspaper: Saving Journalism in
     the Information Age*, University of Missouri Press
88   http://www.newmuseum.org/exhibitions/428/
89   http://www.theregister.co.uk/2009/02/12/google_buys_defunct_paper_mill/
90   http://www.theaustralian.com.au/business/media/
     google-dubbed-internet-parasite/story-e6frg996-1225696931547
91   http://www.shirky.com/writings/information_price.html
92   http://vimeo.com/3723412
93   http://jimmywales.com/2009/10/21/is-the-magazine-dead/
94   http://news.bbc.co.uk/2/hi/asia-pacific/3031716.stm
95   http://www.indyweek.com/indyweek/deserted-moon/Content?oid=1194937
96   http://newsosaur.blogspot.com/2009/05/finally-someone-makes-
     hyperlocal-pay.html
97   http://www.timeinc.com/pressroom/detail.php?id=releases/03182009.php
98   http://nytimes-roulette.appspot.com/
99   http://www.guardian.co.uk/media/pda/2010/mar/30/
     digital-media-algorithms-reporting-journalism
100 http://infolab.northwestern.edu/projects/stats-monkey/
101 http://www.narrativescience.com
102 http://casualdata.com/newsknitter/
103 http://www.thespoof.com/news/spoof.cfm?headline=s4i28539
104 http://thequickbrown.com
105 http://turbulence.org/blog/2008/11/25/time-slip-by-antoine-schmitt/
106 Murphie, A. (2008) 'Ghosted Publics' in *The Mag.net reader 3 -
     Processual Publishing. Actual Gestures*, OpenMute
107 http://newsmap.jp
108 http://www.fallingtimes.info
109 McLuhan, *Understanding Media*, p. 173
110 Sellen and Harper, op. cit., pp. 101, 201
111 Muller, N. and Ludovico, A. (2008) 'Of Process and Gestures: A Publishing Act'
     in *The Mag.net reader 3 - Processual Publishing. Actual Gestures*, OpenMute, p. 6
112 Landow, op. cit.
113 Ilich, F. and Sollfrank, C. 'Another Culture is Possible – not Impossible!' in *The
     Mag.net reader 3 - Processual Publishing. Actual Gestures*, OpenMute, p. 72
114 http://helmutsmits.nl/public-spaces/pamphlet
115 http://www.wdka.nl/news.asp?articleid=
     810&lng=en#u3peq4H3IEUCAl28T7Ve0PE4-0

116 http://www.bookcrossing.com/
117 http://everything2.com/title/Xerox%25209700
118 http://advantage.amazon.com/gp/vendor/public/join
119 http://www.fedex.com/us/office/online-printing.html?OMD157&site= FederatedMedia&value1=EyeBlasterDisplay
120 http://computerworld.co.nz/news.nsf/spec/ 7267B4A516A99D3FCC25755E00826F31
121 http://www.crowdbooks.com/
122 http://en.wikipedia.org/wiki/Espresso_Book_Machine
123 http://www.scribd.com/doc/15576150/1893-March-25-Newark-Daily-Advocate-Newark-OH-Pa-Leo-Future
124 http://artsbeat.blogs.nytimes.com/2009/03/12/ gutenberg-is-dead-long-live-gutenberg/?hp
125 http://us.cnn.com/2009/TECH/04/06/print.on.demand.publishing/index.html
126 http://booktwo.org/notebook/vanity-press-plus-the-tweetbook/
127 http://bookapp.com/tb/connect.php
128 http://www.betternouveau.com/tweetghetto/poster/
129 http://vimeo.com/16889815
130 http://www.fionabanner.com/vanitypress/book11/index.htm
131 http://www.nytimes.com/2004/04/05/business/05reason.html
132 http://www.nytimes.com/2007/06/25/business/media/25adco.html
133 http://postspectacular.com/process/20080711 faberfindslaunch
134 http://www.friezefoundation.org/commissions/detail/per_oskar_leu/
135 http://writtenimages.net/
136 http://www.nytimes.com/2008/04/14/business/media/14link.html
137 http://en.flossmanuals.net
138 http://www.booki.cc/
139 http://ospublish.constantvzw.org/
140 http://blog.welovecolophon.com/
141 http://www.magazinelibrary.jp
142 http://www.magnation.com
143 http://www.stackmagazines.com
144 http://newsgrist.typepad.com/underbelly/2009/05/ abes-penny-a-new-micropublication.html
145 http://issuu.com/amsterdamweekly/docs/amsterdamweekly_issue13_27march
146 http://bitchmagazine.org/post/bitchs-fate-is-in-your-hands
147 http://www.theremediproject.com/projects/issue10/movengen/
148 http://swai.signwave.co.uk
149 http://www.letterror.com/foundry/beowolf/
150 Uzanne and Robida, op. cit.
151 http://www.economist.com/node/21530075
152 http://www2.parc.com/hsl/projects/gyricon/
153 http://en.wikipedia.org/wiki/Electronic_paper
154 http://www.i4u.com/30269/ asus-dual-panel-concept-notebook-suddenly-dual-page-ebook-reader
155 http://articles.businessinsider.com/2009-01-30/ tech/30068072_1_amazon-kindle-delivery-costs-open-letter
156 http://www.thedailybeast.com/newsweek/2007/11/17/ the-future-of-reading.html
157 Carpenter, E. S. (1960) *Marshall McLuhan, Explorations in Communication: an Anthology*, Beacon Press, p. 182

158   http://venturebeat.com/2010/04/30/tablets-book-marketing/

159   http://techcrunch.com/2010/10/22/obama-signing-ipad/?utm_
source=feedburner&utm_medium=feed&utm_campaign=Feed%3A+
Techcrunch+%28TechCrunch%29

160   http://www.youtube.com/watch?v=pzSzKAtfJNg&feature=player_embedded

161   http://radar.oreilly.com/2010/01/2009-oreilly-ebook-revenue-
up-104-percent.html

162   Stallman, R.M., 'Can freedom withstand e-books?' in *Communications
of the ACM*, March 2001

163   http://boingboing.net/2009/07/17/amazon-zaps-purchase.html,
http://boingboing.net/2009/07/23/jeff-bezoss-kindle-a.html

164   http://boingboing.net/2009/07/23/bezos-apologizes-for.html

165   http://www.theglobeandmail.com/news/arts/
meet-publishers-enemy-no-1-cory-doctorow/article1362457/

166   Desai D. D., Hamlin J. C. and Mattson, R. (2010) *History as Art, Art as History:
Contemporary Art and Social Studies Education*, Routledge

167   http://www.observer.com/2011/06/
new-york-times-candle-brings-you-the-sweet-scent-of-ink/

168   http://theoffice.wikia.com/wiki/The_Injury

169   http://smellofbooks.com

170   Calvino, I. (1981) *If On a Winter's Night a Traveller*, Harvest

171   http://gizmodo.com/5504896/there-was-another-iPad-20-year-ago

172   http://www.youtube.com/watch?v=JBEtPQDQNcI

173   Uzanne and Robida, op. cit.

174   http://www.guardian.co.uk/technology/2010/apr/11/
ipad-rusbridger-future-of-the-press

175   http://vimeo.com/10253564

176   http://www.guardian.co.uk/media/pda/2010/mar/19/magazines-ipad

177   http://www.youtube.com/watch?v=ntyXvLnxyXk&feature=player_embedded

178   http://www.psfk.com/2010/03/eye-tracking-technology-may-revolutionize-
the-written-word.html

179   Mod, C., 'Books in the Age of the iPad'; http://craigmod.com/journal/
iPad_and_books/

180   Sellen and Harper, op. cit., p. 8

181   Landow, op. cit., pp. 1-48

182   http://en.wikipedia.org/wiki/Help:Books

183   http://pediapress.com

184   http://www.readability.com/

185   http://readefine.anirudhsasikumar.net/desktop.html

186   http://www.maria-fischer.com/en/traumgedanken_en.html

187   McLuhan, M. (1962) *The Gutenberg Galaxy*, University of Toronto Press, p. 1

188   http://www.sarahcharlesworth.net/series.php?album_id=34

189   http://googleblog.blogspot.com/2009/09/
read-news-fast-with-google-fast-flip.html

190   http://cultureandcommunication.org/deadmedia/index.php/
Newspaper_via_Radio_Facsimile

191   http://bergcloud.com/littleprinter/

192   http://techon.nikkeibp.co.jp/english/NEWS_EN/20090930/175812/

193   http://www.feedjournal.com

194   http://www.theblogpaper.co.uk

195   http://craigmod.com/journal/ipad_and_books/

196   http://en.wikipedia.org/wiki/EPUB
197   http://www.economist.com/node/9231860?story_id=9231860
198   http://www.nytimes.com/2008/01/20/world/asia/20japan.html
199   http://web.archive.org/web/20080212081200/
      http://www.etext.org/index.shtml
200   http://a.parsons.edu/~linf/projects/beyond/statement.html
201   http://www.ew.com/ew/article/0,,304389,00.html
202   http://www.pdf-mags.com
203   http://issuu.com
204   http://www.mstand.com/
205   http://www.exacteditions.com/
206   http://thepiratebay.org/browse/601/0/7
207   http://pirates-of-the-amazon.com
208   http://en.wikipedia.org/wiki/Portable_Document_Format
209   http://en.wikipedia.org/wiki/FlashPaper
210   http://www.scribd.com
211   http://plustek.com/usa/products/opticbook-series/
212   http://www.atiz.com/
213   http://www.qipit.com
214   http://www.ponoko.com/design-your-own/products/scandock-2703
215   http://1dollarscan.com
216   http://en.wikipedia.org/wiki/Handwriting_recognition
217   http://www.fontifier.com
218   http://blog.mimoco.com/?cat=19
219   http://www.cs.cornell.edu/home/kleinber/kdd09-quotes.pdf
220   http://www.designondeadline.com/digitalnewsstand/index.html
221   http://wordflashreader.sourceforge.net
222   Lissitzky-Küppers, S. (1968) *El Lissitzky: life, letters, texts*,
      Thames and Hudson, p. 355
223   http://blog.modernmechanix.com/2008/12/02/
      canned-libraries-open-new-vistas-to-readers/
224   http://en.wikipedia.org/wiki/Bookwheel
225   *Chicago Sunday Tribune*, February 1, 1959, p. 10
226   http://derrickbostrom.com/bostrom/2008/02/12/1975-and-the-changes-to-
      come/; http://aphelis.net/libraries-forced-use-computers-barach-1962/
227   http://en.wikipedia.org/wiki/Bookmobile
228   http://www.archive.org/texts/bookmobile.php
229   http://www.boston.com/news/local/massachusetts/
      articles/2009/09/04/a_library_without_the_books/?page=full
230   http://www.nytimes.com/2009/10/15/books/15libraries.html?_r=2&hp
231   http://www.dailyprincetonian.com/2009/09/28/23918/
232   http://www.buildingways.com/work.html
233   http://www.robotlab.de/bios/bible_engl.htm
234   http://www.corriere.it/politica/09_settembre_07/libro_canada_
      berlusconi_38ca792a-9bd8-11de-88f0-00144f02aabc.shtml
235   http://www.visionaireworld.com
236   http://www.thehumanprinter.org
237   http://www.publishersweekly.com/pw/by-topic/columns-and-blogs/
      cory-Doctorow/article/15883-Doctorow-s-project-with-a-little-help.html
238   http://torrentfreak.com/best-selling-author-turns-piracy-into-profit-080512/
239   http://torrentfreak.com/dan-browns-the-lost-symbol-bestseller-on-bittorrent-090917/

240 Lessig, L. (2008) *Remix. Making Art and Commerce Thrive in the Hybrid Economy*, Bloomsbury

241 http://wordperhect.net/

242 http://vimeo.com/4116727

243 http://timdevin.com/emailflyerproject.html

244 http://web.media.mit.edu/~marcelo/paper/index.html

245 Branwyn, op. cit.

246 http://web.archive.org/web/20081019212050/ http://www.dishwasherpete.com/

247 http://www.alexa.com/siteinfo/boingboing.net

248 *The Mag.net reader 3 - Processual Publishing. Actual Gestures*, OpenMute

249 http://www.xerox.com/innovation/news-stories/erasable-paper/enus.html

250 http://www.nyu.edu/projects/xdesign/mainmenu/archive_stump.html

251 http://www.saveaswwf.com/en/

252 http://www.ecofont.eu

253 http://www.yankodesign.com/2010/02/23/pencil-printer-part-two/

254 http://www.etsy.com/shop/recycledideas?section_id=5477960

255 http://inhabitat.com/laser-cut-leaves-are-natures-unique-business-cards/

256 Graham-Rowe, D., 'Repackaging Data could Double Internet Speed' in *New Scientist #2676*, October 4, 2008

257 Cox, B., 'Foot Prints' in *Eye 70/08*

258 Gleick, J. (2011) *The Information: A History, a Theory, a Flood*, Pantheon

259 Rifkin, J. (2001) *The Age of Access: The New Culture of Hypercapitalism, Where all of Life is a Paid-For Experience*, Tarcher, pp. 76-93, 100

260 http://searchenginewatch.com/article/2053117/Google-Buys-Digital-Historical-Newspaper-Archives-from-PaperofRecord.com

261 http://online.wsj.com/article/ SB10001424052748703701004575113511364939130.html

262 http://www.zimo.co/2011/04/08/live-share-conference-beograd-day-2/

263 http://www.wdl.org/en/

264 http://blog.archive.org/2011/09/17/3-million-texts-for-free/

265 http://www.smartmobs.com/2007/05/25/ humans-helping-out-book-scanners/

266 http://www.post-gazette.com/pg/07175/796164-96.stm

267 http://blog.archive.org/2011/06/06/ why-preserve-books-the-new-physical-archive-of-the-internet-archive/

268 ibid.

269 http://www.libraryjournal.com/article/CA6639703.html

270 http://en.wikipedia.org/wiki/Library.nu

271 http://aaaaarg.org

272 http://www.playboyarchive.com

273 http://rosettaproject.org/

274 Simonite, T. and Le Page, M., 'Digital doomsday: the end of knowledge' in *New Scientist #2745*, February 2, 2010

275 Borges, J. L. (1962) *The Library of Babel*, Grove Press

276 ibid.

277 McLuhan, *Understanding Media*

278 http://english.utah.edu/eclipse/projects/LANGUAGE/language.html

279 http://psrf.detritus.net/

280 Rifkin, op. cit.

281 http://www.diybookscanner.org/

282   http://www.nytimes.com/ref/membercenter/nytarchive.html

283   Batchen, G. (2006) 'The Art of Archiving' in Nicolau, R. *Fotografia na Arte: De Ferramenta a Paradigma (Art and Photography)*, Serralves Museum of Contemporary Art/Público, pp. 138-141

284   McLuhan, Understanding Media

285   http://www.codytrepte.com/1-year-of-archived-email/

286   http://www.timschwartz.org/card-catalog/

287   http://www.rob-matthews.com/index.php?/project/wikipedia/

288   http://www.galerie-vallois.com/artistes/mike-bouchet.html++/image/ bouchet_25_almost_every_city_book.jpg/

289   Garvey, E.G. (2004) 'Scissorizing and Scrapbooks: Nineteenth-Century Reading, Remaking, and Recirculating', in Gitelman L. and Pingree G.B., *New Media, 1740-1915*, The MIT Press

290   ibid.

291   ibid.

292   O'Neil, M. (2009) Cyberchiefs: Autonomy and Authority in Online Tribes, Pluto Press

293   ibid.

294   Curran, J. and Seaton, J. (1997) Power Without Responsibility: the Press and Broadcasting in Britain, Routledge, p. 8

295   ibid, p. 12

296   http://stampamusicale.altervista.org/Insekten%20sekte/index.htm

297   http://en.wikipedia.org/wiki/Associated_Press

298   http://en.wikipedia.org/wiki/Profane_Existence

299   http://www.grrrlzines.net

300   Alferj and Mazzone, op. cit., pp. 29-38

301   http://magnet-ecp.org/

302   Eraso, M., Ludovico, A. and Krekovic, S. (2006) *The Mag.net Reader, experiences in electronic cultural publishing*, Arteleku-Diputación Foral de Gipuzkoa

303   http://web.archive.org/web/20100123215024/ http://magazines.documenta.de/frontend/

304   http://transform.eipcp.net/correspondence/1184160172

305   http://archiv.documenta.de/1389.html?&L=1

306   http://en.wikipedia.org/wiki/Documenta_12_magazines

307   http://www.moreismore.net/

308   http://timdevin.com/ileftthishereforyoutoread-news.html

309   http://freewords.org/fwabout.html

310   http://www.coolhunting.com/culture/namelessletter.php

311   http://www.psfk.com/2009/11/pics-decapitator-x-rolling-stone.html

312   http://techland.time.com/2011/04/20/are-you-ready-to-go-all-digital/

313   http://flipboard.com/

314   http://www.pulse.me/

Onomatopee 77: Cabinet Project
Post-Digital Print — *The Mutation of Publishing since 1894*
ISBN: 978-94-91677-01-4
First edition   (05 – 2012)
Second edition   (03 – 2013)

Text: Alessandro Ludovico

Afterword by: Florian Cramer

Design: Eric de Haas (TheNewStudio)

Heavy editing: Joe Monk, Monastic Language, Rotterdam

Made possible by:
Kenniscentrum Creating 010, Hogeschool Rotterdam
Piet Zwart Institute, Willem de Kooning Academy, Rotterdam

Printer: Lecturis, Eindhoven

Project manager:
Florian Cramer
Ellen Zoete

Edition: 1500
© 2012 the author

Onomatopee
Bleekstraat 23
5611 VB Eindhoven

Creating 010
Instituut voor Onderzoek en Innovatie
Hogeschool Rotterdam
Museumpark 40
3015 CX Rotterdam

408706